# FAITHFUL *fit* & FABULOUS

CONNIE E. SOKOL

# FAITHFUL *fit* & FABULOUS

*get* BACK TO BASICS AND TRANSFORM YOUR LIFE *in* JUST 8 WEEKS!

BONNEVILLE BOOKS
SPRINGVILLE, UTAH

ISBN 13: 978-1-59955-903-2

Published by Bonneville Books, an imprint of Cedar Fort, Inc., 2373 W. 700 S., Springville, UT 84663
Distributed by Cedar Fort, Inc., www.cedarfort.com

LIBRARY OF CONGRESS CATALOGING-IN-PUBLICATION DATA

Sokol, Connie E. author.
Faithful, fit, and fabulous : get back to basics and transform your life—in just 8 weeks! / Connie E. Sokol.
p. cm.
Summary: Uses humor, personal examples, and real-life experiences to teach women how to refresh their daily lives.
Includes bibliographical references.
ISBN 978-1-59955-903-2
1. Mormon women--Conduct of life. 2. Women--Time management. 3. Motherhood--Religious aspects--Church of Jesus Christ of Latter-day Saints. I. Title.
BX8641.S637 2011
248.8'43--dc23

2011018351

Cover design by Danie Romrell
Cover design © 2011 by Lyle Mortimer
Edited and typeset by Kelley Konzak

Printed in the United States of America

10 9 8 7 6 5 4 3 2 1

Printed on acid-free paper

for my beautiful, scrumptious family.

Thank you for helping me stay grounded in love and joy
and to daily relish what matters most.

## other books by connie sokol

*Life Is Too Short for One Hair Color*

*Life Is Too Short for Sensible Shoes*

# contents

# acknowledgments

Writing a book is like birthing a baby. And raising it. And nervously sending it off to college, marriage, and adulthood without your hovering involvement. It's exhilarating and terrifying at the same time.

There are so many to thank for this breathless ride. My Heavenly Father, who, for many years and in diverse ways, has given me ideas, opened unexpected doors, blessed me with amazing people, and provided astounding energy for me to bring this book, and those before it, to fruition. And all while allowing me to keep my family first. It continues to boggle my mind.

To my precious family—David, Ben, Cameron, Ethan, Chelsea, Chloe, and Sophie—for their love, support, and willingness to be guinea pigs in testing "basic" principles and practices, and whose joy in my success and desire to help makes every experience purposeful and memorable. To my fabulous mother, Kinsey Miller, for her pivotal early reading and writing example, continual nudging, and loaning of her beach house for a week to produce the rough of this book.

To the high-quality Cedar Fort Publishing team for their collective belief in this project and an unfinished manuscript. Thank you for seeing the diamond in the rough.

To the amazing BYU Babes of almost twenty-five years—Annie Rollins, Judy Albrecht, and Wendy Clegg—whose thoughts on a girls' weekender sparked the idea for a compilation of a "basics" book. Your support, patience, and beautiful lives have lifted, shaped, and defined me. And for other dear friends, not specifically named, for your inspiring example, loving friendship, and endless patience in listening to intense, life-changing talk when you probably just wanted to do lunch.

To my critique group—particularly Rachael Renee Anderson and Braden Bell—for generously giving of their time, talents, knowledge, and wisdom. Your contributions have been incalculable. This book would never have been what it needed to be without your deft skills and insightful comments.

To my wonderful alpha readers—Amy Chandler, Lisa Hartle, Nicole Kummala, Jill Holmes, Judi Van Leeuwen, and Kinsey Miller—and just as wonderful beta readers—Amy Collins, Angela Ingo, Rebecca Talley, and Tanya Harmon. Your excitement, willingness, and feedback were invaluable.

To the incredible women who assisted me with LIFEChange and other early endeavors. You helped forge a solid foundation on which *Faithful, Fit, and Fabulous* could be built.

To the phenomenal women who continue to attend my presentations (having endured the early ones): you laugh in all the right places, overlook the gaps, and make me feel capable when I would otherwise feel petrified.

To the Anglesey and Richardson families, who graciously allowed me to type in their homes while my daughters did ballet and art lessons. With limited writing time, your hospitality literally made this book possible.

Filled to overflowing, my heart is a bucket of gratitude. Thank you to everyone who has loved, nurtured, and supported me along the way. You've all given shape to my desire to help women and families feel greater joy, peace, and fulfillment.

# introduction

You've chosen this book for a reason. Most likely, you've been living life a certain way and something isn't working. Now you're ready to do it differently—you're getting off the emotional couch, putting away the cheesecake (temporarily), and getting down to business. Maybe it's a matter of organizing the kitchen, getting back into shape, regaining control of your finances, or simply tolerating your evil coworker.

Whatever the reason, you're ready for a change.

Years ago, I needed a big change. After having four children in six years, I had reached my limit spiritually, physically, and emotionally. Tired of feeling overwhelmed—and like a bloated walrus—I took charge of my life. Praying for specific direction, I felt inspired to create the "Year of the Change," a full twelve months dedicated to the very things listed above (minus the evil coworker).

By using a spiritual approach to temporal problems, I found "great treasures of hidden knowledge" (D&C 89:19). Heavenly Father helped me progress. From scriptural principles, I created a personal plan for my ideal life. I also eliminated nasty emotional food triggers—ultimately losing twenty-five pounds and four sizes. Learning and using simple organization skills, I streamlined cooking, cleaning, chore charts, and children's skills to save *twenty-six hours a week*. With that saved time, I wrote and spoke about applying these key principles.

I didn't do any of this perfectly or beautifully—not by a long shot. While exercising, my four young children jumped on my stomach (which I counted as sit-ups). My husband and I had creative discussions about how to implement the changes. And the new routines were not suddenly embraced by adoring and enthusiastic children.

However, I kept at it, "line upon line, precept upon precept" (D&C 98:12). Over several months, I saw good, then great, then amazing changes. Even now I'm reaping the fruits of those early seeds through a generally joyful and organized lifestyle.

I have found I'm not alone. As a speaker for over fifteen years, I've connected with many women and found that we all struggle in some way with similar issues—how to get life back to center and stay focused on what matters most. Unfortunately, many times we fully embrace spiritual guidance only when our "talk show" answers have failed.

*Faithful, Fit, and Fabulous* is about seeking and using true principles with practical solutions.

It is not the eleventh commandment. I am not an expert, and this is not the final how-to. Instead, *Faithful, Fit, and Fabulous* is about enjoyable weekly goals that put eternal principles into play. It's about taking control of life and feeling joy—the joy we've been told we're here to experience.

You *can* feel happy and organized and fit. You can serve without feeling it's a burden. You can have financial peace and prosperity. You can pursue personal purpose and develop talents in things that delight you. As we patiently practice key scripture principles, Heavenly Father can fully assist us in creating a life full of purposeful experiences—both hoped for and unexpected. I know this is true. I have experienced this assistance in my own life and have witnessed it in the lives of others.

Remember, this is your life and your book. Don't waste time writing cardboard answers or comments. Instead, dig deep within and allow yourself to blossom. Discover who you are and what you are to do.

"They that wait upon the Lord shall renew their strength; they shall mount up with wings as eagles; they shall run, and not be weary; and they shall walk, and not faint" (Isaiah 40:31).

Remember to enjoy the process. All of it matters. All of it counts. Dive deep. Open your soul to His promptings.

Your life is about to change.

## How the Eight-Week Program Works

The goal of *Faithful, Fit, and Fabulous* is to refresh your life with a quick burst of eight goals in eight weeks, one goal in eight key areas of your life. Simple and fun.

For example, with a focused, eight-week approach, you could create a plan similar to the following:

| | Problem Life Area | Weekly Goal |
|---|---|---|
| **Week 1** | Improve a holy habit | Create a sublime spiritual sanctuary |
| **Week 2** | Write a personal life plan | e.g. "I am a loving, spiritually centered, fit, organized, and financially savvy woman who is healthily connected to my loved ones and delights in being there for others." |
| **Week 3** | Incorporate a fit & fab principle | Positive verbal body messages |
| **Week 4** | Create a joyful habit | Resting time for mom—30 mins. daily |
| **Week 5** | Organize one facet of family life | Clean and organize the garage |
| **Week 6** | Connect with my family | Positively handle a difficult situation |
| **Week 7** | Be more balanced in motherhood | Set up cleaning zones for children's chores |
| **Week 8** | Secure financial peace | Create and use a realistic budget |

Eight solid goals under your belt—and that's in just eight weeks!

## Beginning the Eight-Week Program

The *Faithful, Fit, and Fabulous* format is simple. *Each week* you will read a different chapter and set a goal. Then you will achieve it, review it, and reward yourself for it.

**Step 1: Read the beginning two chapters.** The only requirement is to start with chapter one in the first week and chapter two in the second week. These two sections create a solid foundation for the rest of the book. After those two weeks, feel free to choose any chapter in any order. Each chapter focuses on a key life area (for example, organization, fitness, or balance in motherhood), shares clear principles, and gives real-life applications. Whatever your situation—married, single, divorced—apply the content in a way that works best for you.

Note: All of the principles and most resources have been taken directly from general conference talks, lesson manuals, Church magazines, and other Church-approved materials.

**Step 2: Choose a Weekly Goal, review it, and reward it.** Each week you will read a chapter, set a Weekly Goal, and choose a personal reward. At the end of the week, you will review your progress.

Each week's goal is unrelated to the next, so generally choose a one-time goal (for example, complete a project, eliminate a negative habit, or prepare for a new habit). For example, chapter one is about Holy Habits. A one-time goal might be to create a spiritual sanctuary. If you choose a continuing goal, that's fine too, but maintaining that goal would not be your focus. You would still move on to another chapter the following week. Remember, this is an eight-week jump start of your life. You can come back and go deep with any of your goals at a later time.

To easily record your Weekly Goal information, use the provided Post-It Page (found in the chapter "Back to Basics: More!" or download it at www.8basics.com). Print a new Post-It Page weekly and write your life paragraph, Weekly Goal, and reward. (Note: "Holy Habits" is the only chapter for which you won't write your life plan because you will not have completed it yet). At the end of the week, review your goal using the provided questions on the page.

Post goal pages on your wall, planner, or fridge. If you're like me, half of my goal-achieving battle is remembering what I'm working on!

Just a note about a reward: it's a *vital* part of goal setting and yet is the most difficult one for women to practice. A reward is key to rewiring positive feelings about goals. Even if the goal isn't completed, acknowledge your efforts. One woman paid herself five dollars for each workout and put it toward a new outfit. Rewards don't have to be a big production, but they do need to be meaningful to you. Select something you can't wait to do—read a book, do lunch with a friend, or enroll in a hobby class.

**Step 3: Continue to choose a chapter and set a goal!** *Faithful, Fit, and Fabulous* is that easy. Simply read a chapter and a set a goal each week for eight weeks. Complete the book as you like—a little at soccer, some more at dance—stopping and returning where and when you want.

In each chapter, I've provided easy, thought-juicing activities called "Back to Basics—Go!" They help you get in, knead the dough, and let it rise. Help children and spouses understand that you need time to complete these activities. Tell them that mom is doing her homework so they can clean their own bathroom.

Ideally, you will choose a fairly consistent time during the week to read and complete a chapter (for example, Sunday evening). If possible, create a personal sanctuary (even if it's a corner in your bedroom) to make it more appealing.

## A Week in the Program at a Glance

Take a look at the program as if you were doing it right now.

1. **Read a chapter.** To begin, do the first two chapters in two weeks and then choose any chapter per week after that. Complete the "Back to Basics—Go!" activities in each area *as you desire.*
2. **Choose one Weekly Goal.** Prayerfully choose a goal that stretches but doesn't overwhelm. Then go to work.
3. **Achieve your goal and reward yourself.** Give your best energy for one week and then enjoy rewarding your efforts.
4. **Complete your review.** At the end of the week, answer three quick questions to tweak the next week's goal for even better results.
5. **Set a new goal.** Repeat the same fabulous rhythm: choose another exciting chapter and set a new Weekly Goal.

There it is, simple and enjoyable! To give you goal-setting ideas, each chapter includes suggestions for Weekly Goals. As you move forward, you can feel Heavenly Father's tender mercies inspire you to achieve, even in the midst of a chaotic life. At the end of eight weeks, you will have accomplished eight substantial, life-changing goals or projects.

If you have any questions, feel free to email me at connie@8basics.com. I'm here to help and hopefully connect you with other women, wisdom, and Faithful, Fit, and Fabulous ideas.

You've got the tools. Are you ready to juice up your life? Let's go!

*one*

# establish holy habits

"Spirituality yields two fruits. The first is inspiration to know what to do. The second is power, or the capacity to do it."

Elder Richard G. Scott

Several years ago, I was asked to be the host of a new radio show for women in Utah. The problem? They wanted me full time, from 3 to 6 p.m. My first gut instinct was to say no. I had several children and had made it a priority to be an at-home mother. But a feeling inside encouraged me to meet with them before I turned it down. Confused, I spent those days praying, reading scriptures, tossing and turning, and in tears. My desire to share life-changing concepts didn't trump wanting to be home with my family. So I listened for the Spirit and sought for peace.

One day I was reading in the scriptures about the brother of Jared building barges. In response to his building concerns, the Lord asks *him* what to do about light in the vessels. He goes on to patiently outline specific dangers to consider (Ether 2:23) before going on to say:

"And behold, I prepare you against these things; for ye cannot cross this great deep save I prepare you against the waves of the sea, and the winds which have gone forth, and the floods which shall come. Therefore, what will ye that I should prepare for you?" (Ether 2:25).

That resonated with me. Instead of wringing my hands, I went to my knees and outlined concerns and possible solutions. Feeling more peaceful, I still had no confirmed plan—even after a priesthood blessing—but felt confident enough to at least move forward.

At the meeting, I jumped in with both feet and explained that I wouldn't be able to do all they wanted. However, I could manage two days a week, from 12 to 3 p.m. It felt right. Instantly, the two interviewers looked at each other, and one of them said, "Job share!" As it turned out, another possible host had rejected the 3–6 p.m. time slot because she also had children at home. The "job share" concept became the show template. Rather than one host, there were three of us—all part-time, with a schedule benefiting our individual families.

Without that instruction, peace, and confirmation from prayer, scriptures, and personal promptings, I would not have had that brief but pivotal radio experience in my life.

In this chapter, we'll go deep with three Holy Habits: prayer, scripture study, and personal promptings. Using all three habits together, we can experience life-changing awareness of the Lord's answers to problems and feel greater peace.

In an LDS general conference address, Elder Dallin H. Oaks shared this insight:

> We conclude that the final Judgment is not just an evaluation of a sum total of good and evil acts—what we have done. It is an acknowledgment of the final effect of our acts and thoughts—what we have become. It is not enough for anyone just to go through the motions. The commandments, ordinances, and covenants of the gospel are not a list of deposits required to be made in some heavenly account. The gospel of Jesus Christ is a plan that shows us how to become what our Heavenly Father desires us to become.[1]

## Prayer, Scriptures, and Personal Promptings

My husband and I once took a scuba diving class together. During one lesson, we were taught to skin dive. This difficult dive involves taking three or four quick breaths, holding the last one, then diving and re-ascending when you need more air. For safety, the dive is done while a buddy watches from the water surface through a mask and snorkel.

Before our dive, the instructor told us that a week earlier, a fit military man was skin diving at the very place we would be certifying. He was skin diving for four minutes at a time, rather than just one or two, and using eight or nine quick breaths, rather than the safety rule of three or four. Although he had no diving buddy, a scuba diving class that was also present randomly watched him. After surfacing from his first ascent, the man immediately took another eight or nine quick breaths and dove again. Ascending from the second dive, he apparently came within five feet of the surface, blacked out, and drowned. All the while, the class not associated with him was unaware of what was happening.

Though there may have been other factors at play, our teacher emphasized respect for rules and how casualness about safety could lead to tragedy.

For me, this is a paradigm for prayer, scriptures, and personal promptings. We know what they are, we know they're effective, and yet we get casual. We think we can dive without them.

Although we may understand why prayer, scripture study, and personal promptings are essential, sometimes we aren't consistent. Why is that?

## What Keeps Us from Holy Habits?

Most often what keeps us from spiritual sustenance isn't a lack of testimony—it's busy schedules with callings, children's activities, work, volunteering, or sheer exhaustion. Whatever the reason, our consistency with these important habits suffers. Let's look at three of the most common obstacles and a way to overcome each of them.

### *Busyness*

Being constantly on the go is not only frustrating it's also draining—both spiritually and physically. To borrow a phrase, we are ever carpooling but never closer to the truth.

Ultimately, busyness can lead to becoming spiritually casual. In a recent general conference, Elder Dale G. Renlund shared a life-changing experience. During early married life, he worked at a hospital, and his shift included Sundays. His busy schedule made church attendance and scripture study difficult. One Sunday after a long shift, instead of attending church with his family he went home to take a much-needed nap. When he couldn't sleep, he began questioning why his testimony had lost its zeal. He realized that because of his schedule—where day blended into night—he would fall asleep before praying or reading the scriptures.[2]

Has that happened to you? Think of nursing a baby—day blending into night, walking around in a milky haze. We've been there, done that. But after a while, even in that "justifiable" situation, the lack of routine saps our spiritual reserves, leaving us physically and spiritually lethargic.

Elder Renlund shared an inspiring solution. He got off the couch, asked for forgiveness, and then made a promise to the Lord that day, and every day following, to pray morning and night and read the scriptures. Within a few weeks, his testimony zeal had returned, along with the promise to never get caught in that casual cycle again.[3] If your obstacle is busyness or being casual, get serious and put it on your planner.

### *Not Trusting His Promises*

Most women I meet are working double time to ensure their worthiness before the Lord. Ironically, these same women don't claim the blessings they've "earned." The Lord Himself has said, "I, the Lord, am bound when ye do what I say; but when ye do not what I say, ye have no promise" (D&C 82:10).

The Lord has promised that if we do what He asks, He will lead our lives for good—to what is best for us in the eternities. His promises are sure.

In an LDS general conference talk, Elder Spencer J. Condie invited us to claim the following promises:

- The Lord will undo our heavy burdens
- The Holy Ghost will be our constant companion
- We will receive divine guidance and inspiration
- What we ask the Father in the name of Jesus Christ will be given to us[4]

These incredible promises are ours for the asking! That means we need to step up, kneel down, and ask in faith that we be given what we've done our very best to receive—even though we're not perfect.

Too often we reach *out there* for solutions, believing in a magical fix to gain more time, energy—just more something. But we don't need to look to media or a person of the week. The simple holy habits of prayer, scripture study, and listening to personal promptings will lead us to custom-made answers.

***Changes in Routine, Distractions, and Everything Else***

You're praying, reading scriptures, and moving along fabulously. Then it happens. You have a baby, a child gets sick, your husband's workload doubles, or the holidays hit. Suddenly, that beautiful routine that kept you focused is gone.

Awareness is nine-tenths of the law. So be aware that life's transitions will inevitably attempt to thwart holy habits. Let's look at some ways to replenish our spiritual reservoirs.

## Prayer

The Bible Dictionary says, "As soon as we learn the true relationship in which we stand toward God (namely, God is our Father, and we are His children), then at once prayer becomes natural and instinctive on our part" (Bible Dictionary, s.v. "prayer," 752).

Pray always! It's the first thing to do out of bed or after a shower. Pray in the car, while folding laundry, making dinner, and definitely when talking with a teenager. Prayer is a constant companion—not because of duty but because it brings the comfort of having your closest, wisest friend with you all day, every day.

**1. Plan for opposition.** Poised for prayer, suddenly your child needs lunch money, the dog chews your purse, or the dryer goes on the fritz. When that happens (because it will) smile and know all is going according to plan. If there isn't a little opposition, something isn't right. In the paraphrased words from *Finding Nemo*, just keep praying, just keep praying.

**2. Pray from the heart.** In her book *Lighten Up*, Sister Chieko Okazaki says:

"Heavenly Father doesn't want to hear only 'nice' prayers. He wants to hear real prayers, honest prayers. . . . How many times are our evening prayers just one more chore? . . . But who are we trying to kid? . . . He doesn't want polite platitudes. He wants you! All of you! He wants to be the center of your total life–the worried you, the mad you, and the sad you, as well as the inspired, happy, obedient, loving you."[5]

When we are truly open and respectfully honest with the Lord, our hearts are changed. Too often we seethe about a neighbor, dutifully kneel to bless missionaries, then return to seething about the neighbor. We remain unchanged. But if we open up to Him and share real concerns, praying for the desire to love, for the ability to see from His perspective, we begin to see "things spiritual."

Sister Patricia Holland shares the following from her devotional address "With Your Face to the Son":

"[Prayer] ought not to seem just a convenient and contrived miracle, for if we are to search for real light . . . we have to pray as the ancients prayed. We are women now, not children, and are expected to pray with maturity. The words most often used to describe urgent, prayerful labor are wrestle, plead, cry, and hunger. In some sense, prayer may be the hardest work we will ever be engaged in."[6]

**3. Pray about anything.** Want to like cooking? Need help losing weight? Trying to solve how to do three hours of errands in one and a half? Then pray. Yes, we need to get up and do, but first we ask for help to do it in the best way. I have experienced all three of those situations, and I can testify that it works. Involve Him in your life, in every aspect.

In the book *If Life Were Easy, It Wouldn't Be Hard*, Sister Sheri Dew states that *nothing* is too insignificant to pray about. There is no anxiety, worry, or weakness too small to trouble Him with. And she reminds us that the Lord invites us to weary Him with our requests and needs and seek for His counsel in all things.[7]

## Back to Basics—Go!

Take one minute and write down pressing problems that you would love the Lord to eliminate. Next, choose the toughest issue, the one that keeps you up at night or eating chocolate during the day. Write it on a sticky note or a 3x5 card and place it in your scriptures. Put another copy in your planner or by your bedside. With purpose and focus, pray about the problem. What have you done so far to solve it? What do you need from the Lord? Jot down ideas—and inspiration—and include their outcomes.

**4. Add a devotional.** Even if you're already praying and studying daily, perhaps a particular problem needs a little more help. In his *Ensign* article "Opening the Heavens," Elder Yoshihiko Kikuchi shared the power of a morning devotional. This consists of a few minutes spent quietly with Heavenly Father sharing concerns and waiting for insights. Although initially tailored to missionaries, the principle is applicable to all. More than praying, he invites us to rise early, exercise, be clean, kneel in prayer, and wait a bit for inspiration while pondering scriptures, a recent general conference talk, or a specific problem.

When I first read this article, part of me thought, "You're killing me here!" Just reading "rise early" made me take a deep breath. By the time I finished exercising and showering, it would be time for lunch.

Then I took a second look. What ultimately convinced me to try it were the blessings. While Elder Kikuchi served as a mission president, his missionaries practiced morning devotionals. He said that not long afterward, the missionaries received more member referrals, had more teaching opportunities, and doubled and then tripled the number of baptisms in the mission. He recognized that the Holy Ghost had magnified the missionaries' efforts.[8]

Wow. Like those missionaries, I wanted my efforts to be magnified by the Holy Spirit. Although I wouldn't necessarily have the same outcome, I imagined equally important blessings that could come to our family. So I attempted a morning devotional. Yes, it was difficult. In fact, with six children, it was excruciating. I could carve out a miraculous few minutes only two or three times a week (not without interruption or trauma). But over time, my devotionals increased, even on days when it didn't seem feasible.

With notepad in hand, I wrote thoughts and feelings, both at the time and later on. Often I would have many things written, sometimes a few, sometimes none at all. But always I can testify that promptings came at some point in answer to my morning supplications.

To try this, find a quiet place. In a busy household, I know this can be like asking the Red Sea to part. However, if we truly desire communication and inspiration, the Lord will reward us with creativity and insight. The place doesn't have to be fancy. (I have used our clothes closet.) Nor does it have to be a long time. (I've used as little as ten minutes and as long as forty).

Simply give it a try and see what spiritual abundance the Lord will share with you.

## Scriptures

What's your first thought when you see the words "read your scriptures"?

For some people, scriptures have become just another check-off on the to-do list. As a teenager of less-active parents, I remember reading the beginning of 1 Nephi and finding it so unearthly boring that I put it down. Instead, I read Psalms and Proverbs in the Old Testament, which for some reason were more enjoyable. I chose favorite scriptures and wrote them on 3x5 cards—quotables like "He who putteth His trust in the Lord is made fat." (I got a lot of mileage out of that one in college). Or, "It is better to dwell in the corner of the housetop, than with a brawling woman in a wide house." That's one I occasionally still share with my husband.

If we put a little effort into study, we can make the scriptures fabulously exciting again. It's up to us. Just like my teenage experience, we simply need to find a way to make it personal. Perhaps choose from the following ideas.

**1. Juice it up.** So, how do you juice it up? Probably in a different way than you're doing now! No handbook says you must read the scriptures a certain way. Choose a topic that makes you salivate. Put a candy in between each page as you read. Study with your favorite decadent treat. (I love reading with a cup of chamomile herbal tea and butter cookies). We're to feast, so feast! Find a place in your home or apartment and make it The Sublime Place of Savory Scripture Study. Choose a favorite chair with a cozy throw and soft lighting. Make your bedroom a sanctuary again. Get the Lego blocks out of the room—or any other project that doesn't belong in a peaceful and lovely place. Reading the scriptures will become delicious as you feast upon the word and drink from living waters.

**2. Read with a problem or question in mind.** Years ago my husband and I considered switching from his regular employment to becoming self-employed. It was a tough choice. Working for a company provided a reasonable measure of security but lower income. Being self-employed brought more financial opportunity but greater risk. We were just starting out in life, and with two young children, our decision was crucial. As we prayed about the answer, I remember reading 1 Nephi 17:11–16 and feeling that spiritual zing, as if He were

speaking to me: "I will be your light in the wilderness; and I will prepare the way before you, if it so be that ye shall keep my commandments; wherefore, inasmuch as ye shall keep my commandments ye shall be led towards the promised land; and ye shall know that it is by me that ye are led."

The solution was clear: If we would keep His commandments, we would be led. Right after this scripture experience, my husband received an opportunity to go out on his own, and we began our journey to a successful business.

Consider a problem in your life. Refer to it as you read and study the scriptures. When we ask specifically, solutions flow more easily.

Elder Henry B. Eyring shared that when we come to a crisis in our lives, going to the scriptures will make all the difference. As we look for help, we will see that the Lord—who anticipates our needs—has given us direction in the scriptures if we will actively seek it.[9]

**3. Power pack it.** When you combine prayer with scriptures, you'll get a formidable spiritual boost for the day. Sister Cheryl C. Lant once said that to increase her sensitivity to the Spirit, she prays to have it with her as she reads the scriptures. In doing so, she can often see how to make life changes as well as feel the Lord's assurance and strength in helping her to accomplish them.[10]

Each of our situations is different. But the common thread woven through our lives is that scripture study is a powerful tool: we just need to notch it up and make it count.

## Personal Promptings

One day my ten-year-old daughter asked, "When was the last earthquake in Utah?" My teenage son answered, "Oh, we have several a day; we just can't feel them."

Spiritual promptings are like that. We ask when they'll come, but they're already here. We just don't feel them. It's up to us to be more in tune, to know what to look for, and to have the courage to obey.

**1. Be still.** When was the last time you were still (and awake)? Assuming we are living worthily, stillness is key to increasing spiritual listening capacity. Just like exercise, if we don't plan, it won't happen.

Sister Vicki F. Matsumori reminds us that because the Spirit is a still, small voice, it's vital to carve out time daily when we aren't overwhelmed by electronics. We need quiet time daily to give the Spirit an opportunity to whisper direction and give us comfort.[11]

We must make time to be peaceful. Mary Ellen Edmunds once said one of her goals was to stop global whining. The first step is to stop complaining about zero alone-time and actually do something about it. We are the moms. We set the final boundary. If we need to lie down and be still for fifteen minutes, then hang a sign, shut the door, and ignore any family wailing or gnashing of teeth.

Believe me, they will respect you more and bug you less when the message is clear—spiritual things come first. My children know not to bother me in alone-time because my first response is, "Did you clean your bathroom? Bedroom? Kitchen floor? Parakeet cage?" And if that list is complete—miracle notwithstanding—then there is always laundry and matching socks. Suddenly, my children scatter, and everyone gets along just fine.

**2. Understand how the spirit speaks to you.** Elder Boyd K. Packer shares an experience from when his parents were newly married. They lived a difficult farm life, raising both crops and a family on little money. Heading into town one day, his father invited his mother and children to come along. But climbing into the buggy, she hesitated and then declined. When her husband asked what was wrong, she simply replied that she didn't know but had a feeling she shouldn't go.

Understanding what that meant, her husband left the family at home and headed for town, leaving his wife doubting her decision. She had been in the home only moments when she found the ceiling on fire. The children formed a brigade from the pump, and she was able to throw water on the ceiling and put out the fire.

Hidden in their home was their life savings. What could have easily been a tragedy became a spiritually strengthening experience.[12]

The scriptures tell us the fruits of the Spirit include love, joy, longsuffering, temperance, and faith (Galatians 5:22–23). Spiritual promptings can also be in a vision (JS—H 1:17), in our heart and mind (D&C 6:15–16), in the form of a stupor of thought (D&C 9:9), or peace (D&C 6:23).

When we're trying to decipher whether a prompting is our own thought or the Spirit whispering, consider what Elder Richard G. Scott said:

> Actually, He will reply in one of *three* ways. First, you can feel the peace, comfort, and assurance that confirm that your decision is right. Or second, you can sense that unsettled feeling, the stupor of thought, indicating that your choice is wrong. Or third—and this is the difficult one—you can feel no response.
>
> What do you do when you have prepared carefully, have prayed fervently, waited a reasonable time for a response, and still do not feel an answer? You may want to express thanks when that occurs, for it is an evidence of His trust. When you are living worthily and your choice is consistent with the Savior's teachings and you need to act, proceed with trust. As you are sensitive to the promptings of the Spirit, one of two things will certainly occur at the appropriate time: either the stupor of thought will come, indicating an improper choice, or the peace or the burning in the bosom will be felt, confirming that your choice was correct.[13]

**3. Following promptings.** Years ago, I took my two little ones to a nearby park. After they were settled on the slides—located inside a low wall—I sat down briefly on the grass. Enjoying the peace and sunshine, I closed my eyes in a brief prayer of gratitude. I heard a voice inside my mind say, "Chloe."

Immediately, I opened my eyes and turned in time to see my young daughter tearing across the grassy field toward the busy road. Up and running, I called her name several times, but to no avail. I caught her by the shirt right before she reached the road and was able to stop a possible tragedy. This experience taught me not only to continually listen, but to immediately obey.

**4. Keep a promptings journal.** Several years ago, in an effort to better understand the language of the Spirit, I bought a small notebook and began recording what I thought were promptings. On the first day alone, I could hardly write them fast enough. Even more surprising and ridiculous was how often I delayed them—"I'll do that right after I go to the post office and the bank," I would think. Keeping the journal helped me separate what was revelation and what wasn't and learn how to better respond. Today, I combine a gratitude journal with my prompting journal to help me see patterns and express appreciation.

## Wrapping Up

As you consider prayer, scripture study, and personal promptings, I invite you to prayerfully choose one goal for the coming week, whether it's a one-time project or starting a habit. Although this particular week is one baby step in that process, apply your best efforts to get the flywheel humming.

Sister Ann M. Dibb said that the Lord has already given us all we need to successfully return to Him, such as prayer, scriptures, modern-day prophets, and the guidance of the Holy Ghost. Although using the "equipment" may be awkward, inconvenient, or old-fashioned, for proper protection we need to diligently choose to use it.[14]

## Suggested Weekly Goals for Prayer, Scriptures, and Personal Promptings

Choose *one* area, and set *one* goal! Do not set a goal that requires "every day." When you have achieved a goal for at least two or three times a week, then try setting it daily.

### *Prayer*

- Pray morning and night a certain number of days this week.
- Make a prayer card of personal concerns—keep by your bed/planner.
- Pray before reading scriptures (read at least ten to fifteen minutes).

### *Scripture Study*

- Listen to a conference or scripture CD as you drive.
- Create a Scripture Sanctuary in your room, home, or apartment.
- Study five to ten scriptures in the Topical Guide on the Holy Ghost.

### *Promptings*

- Use a spiritual promptings journal—track what you spiritually feel for three to five days.
- Mark key topics with a colored pencil—choose one topic for the week or month.
- Have a morning devotional one or two times this week.
- Match your personal concerns with scripture stories.
- Record a few past spiritual experiences—what brought it to pass, what was the outcome.

## Notes

Quote at chapter start found in Richard G. Scott, "To Acquire Spiritual Guidance," *Ensign*, Nov. 2009, 6–9.

1. Dallin H. Oaks, "The Challenge to Become," *Ensign*, Nov. 2000, 32–34.
2. Dale G. Renlund, "Preserving the Heart's Mighty Change," *Ensign*, Nov. 2009, 98–99.
3. Ibid.
4. Spencer J. Condie, "Claim the Exceeding Great and Precious Promises," *Ensign*, Nov. 2007, 16.
5. Chieko N. Okazaki, *Lighten Up* (Salt Lake City: Deseret Book, 1993), 183.
6. Jeffrey R. Holland and Patricia T. Holland, *On Earth As It Is in Heaven* (Salt Lake City: Deseret Book, 1989), 89.
7. Sheri Dew, *If Life Were Easy, It Wouldn't Be Hard*, (Salt Lake City: Deseret Book, 2005), 133.
8. Yoshihiko Kikuchi, "Opening the Heavens," *Ensign*, Aug. 2009, 34–38.
9. Henry B. Eyring, "A Discussion on Scripture Study." *Ensign*, Jul. 2005, 22.
10. Cheryl C. Lant, "My Soul Delighteth in the Scriptures." *Ensign*, Nov. 2005, 76.
11. Vicki F. Matsumori, "Helping Others Recognize the Whisperings of the Spirit," *Ensign*, Nov. 2009, 10–12.
12. Boyd K. Packer, *Memorable Stories and Parables by Boyd K. Packer* (Salt Lake City: Bookcraft, 1997), 1–3.
13. Richard G. Scott, "Using the Supernal Gift of Prayer," *Ensign*, May 2007, 8–11.
14. Ann M. Dibb, "Hold On," *Ensign*, Nov. 2009, 79–81. Emphasis added.

two

# create a life plan

"We are sons and daughters of an immortal, loving, and all-powerful Father in Heaven. We are created as much from the dust of eternity as we are from the dust of the earth. Every one of us has potential we can scarcely imagine."

Elder Joseph B. Wirthlin

Consider that last phrase: "potential we can scarcely imagine." Are we tapping into it? Sister Patricia T. Holland says:

"Every element of creation has its own purpose and performance, its own divine role and mission. If our desires and works are directed toward what our heavenly parents have intended us to be, we will come to feel our part in their plan . . . and nothing will give us more ultimate peace."[1]

Elder Joseph B. Wirthlin explained the need and privilege to create of our lives a masterpiece.[2] So, how do we reach our potential and create a masterpiece when we're overwhelmed, stretched, and just trying to get through the day?

## Create a Life Plan

A life plan consists of a paragraph detailing your ideal way of life *and* Weekly Goals to achieve it. It's fun and functional. It's a blueprint to help you clarify, focus, and live your ideal life. Rather than a rigid dictation of must-dos, it's more of a flexible and fabulous rubber band.

Having covered Holy Habits in the previous chapter, I invite you to use the tools of prayer, scripture study, and personal promptings to discover your personal purpose and desires. In this chapter you'll create a life plan from start to finish, with great suggestions on how to use it. Let's go!

## What You Want and What the Lord Wants

Knowing what we truly want from life is crucial. Our desires are what we will drift to, seek out, and ultimately focus on. And, as our desires move from what we want to what the Lord wants for us, our lives will become centered and balanced.

Some years ago a local TV channel asked me to do my own television show. By all accounts it seemed tailor-made—an efficient method for sharing life-improving messages.

However, raising six children meant I had a tiny window of time and energy to devote to the program. After stipulating a few parameters, I felt peaceful about taking one morning a week to film the show, while weekly plans and calls would be completed during my daughter's naptime. They agreed, and we moved forward.

A few months of preparation later, the rehearsals began. Immediately, it was clear that even with my preparations, the reality would require more than I could give.

Confused about what to do, I prayed, read the scriptures, and attended the temple several times seeking an answer. I knew that although I would be sharing gospel principles, and could technically make it work (so long as I didn't sleep), this experience didn't fit my personal vision. Doing the show would overload me and my family. Though it was difficult, I ultimately declined, and the producers graciously understood.

When creating a life plan, ask yourself what you want and then, more important, what the Lord wants for you. Life will bring great opportunities, especially in this day and age, to women. But every opportunity is not necessarily in our or our family's best interests. Using Holy Habits and a personal life plan, we remember what is vital and eternal, no matter how tempting the offer.

In this chapter, I will coach you through designing your life plan. This consists of writing a concise paragraph about your ideal life and choosing one goal to begin achieving it. If you already have ideas for these, skip the following brainstorming exercise and go right to "Create a Life Paragraph."

## Brainstorm Your Life Plan

**1. Take a piece of paper and write at the top, "What I Want from My Life."** Write as quickly as you can, filling the paper, if need be. If you're left-brain, set the timer for five minutes. Don't stop to think about what you should or shouldn't write, just put down what is in your heart and soul. Designer Dorothy Draper said, "Don't design scared. Dream."[3] This is your moment to dream about a day in your ideal life. What would your day include? What would it look like? Consider the areas of spiritual, emotional, physical, mental, enjoyable, and so on.

Not sure what to write? Elder Wirthlin gives us ideas of what we can include in our personal life plans: love the Lord with our heart, mind, and strength; join worthy causes; create homes of spiritual strength; magnify callings; continue learning; strengthen our testimonies; and serve others.[4]

If you need additional specifics, consider these questions:

- If money were no object, what would I have/do/be in my life to be happy?
- If I could be with the people I choose, what would my relationships look like?
- If the functional part of my life were taken care of, what interests would I pursue?
- If I took classes in things that interest me or in areas I want to improve in, what would the class topics be?

Allow these thoughts to percolate. Feel free to revise or eliminate answers that don't fit your feelings.

TIP: You may be tempted to skip writing this down. DON'T DO IT! Research shows writing down a chosen goal makes you significantly more likely to succeed. My homebuilder husband uses only the best framers. Why? He says it cuts the work in half because everyone follows the framer. You are framing your life plan. Though it will likely take more writing than any other chapter in this book, it's worth every letter. Every future chapter and personal goal will be so much easier.

**2. Next, turn the paper over and write at the top, "What's Stopping Me?"** Again, write as quickly as you can. After these two exercises, if you're still stumped, take a third paper and write, "What I Don't Want." This eliminates what doesn't belong in your life and clarifies what you desire.

Take a minute and look over what you've written and congratulate yourself. These personal insights are gold!

**3. Last, and most important, ask Heavenly Father what He wants for you.** If you remember from the previous chapter, the brother of Jared introduced us to this key principle. How did he build the barges? He asked the Lord for a solution, then brought his best ideas. How did the Lord respond? He not only touched the stones to give them light, but the Lord actually revealed himself to the brother of Jared too.

Though that will not likely be our experience, using that same key principle, we can bring our figurative sixteen stones—our ideal life description—and ask the Lord what He desires for us. We are commanded "in all things to ask of God"—then the best part—"who giveth liberally" (D&C 46:7). The Lord knows everything: how it will pan out and how you will best flourish. Take your plans to Him. I can promise He has simpler, better, sometimes bigger, but always more wisely prepared plans than you and I could ever choreograph.

So why bother developing your plan and ideas first—why not just let Him tell you from the start? Because the Lord wants us to choose. He does not dictate what we do in this life. Rather, He gives us agency to "prove [us] herewith" (Abraham 3:25). He doesn't want to control our lives, He wants to see what we will make of them when given the opportunity. Even though the Lord commands us to involve Him in our decisions, He does not command our decisions. He says:

> For behold, it is not meet that I should command in all things; for he that is compelled in all things, the same is a slothful and not a wise servant; wherefore he receiveth no reward.
>
> Verily I say, men should be anxiously engaged in a good cause, and do many things of their own free will, and bring to pass much righteousness;
>
> For the power is in them, wherein they are agents unto themselves. And inasmuch as men do good they shall in nowise lose their reward." (D&C 58:26–28)

We must make the first step. If you want a masterpiece of your life, you must pick up the brush and choose a color.

## Create a Life Paragraph

Now that you have a framework, it's time to add enjoyable details. Remember, what you write is not chiseled in stone. It's a working idea for you to continually take to the Lord, the Chief Architect, to discuss, tweak, and enjoy with Him. Using the scriptures, let's create a specific life paragraph and Weekly Goal.

Heavenly Father has a vision. In Moses 1:39, it says, "For behold, this is my work and my glory—to bring to pass the immortality and eternal life of man."

Everything that happens in the Lord's Church—every principle, ordinance, meeting, and activity—should in some way fulfill this ultimate objective. In your life, create a similar umbrella vision, a succinct paragraph that states what you ultimately want from your life. Then create goals and behaviors that support and fulfill that vision.

To do this, consider three main areas of your life: self, relationships, and life skills. To describe these areas, use buzz words—one- or two-word descriptions of what you want from life. Include core values (for example, peace, love, integrity, and joy) since these will bear lasting fruit. For example, your buzz words could include:

**Self:** happiness, peace, energy, vibrant health, purpose
**Relationships:** healthy connection, fun, clear communication
**Life skills:** financial security, organization of time and my home

**Write your life paragraph here using buzz words or phrases to describe your ideal life:**

Self: ______________________________________________

Relationships: _____________________________________

Life skills: ________________________________________

Using buzz words, create five or six full sentences per topic. They might look like this:

**Self:** I am a loving, spiritually centered, happy daughter of God. I am strong inside and out, with energy and joy. I enjoy hobbies that fulfill a personal and creative purpose.

**Relationships:** I connect with family and friends through healthy, positive interactions and communications. I know how to deal with difficult situations and practice those skills. I set appropriate boundaries with those around me, at home or in the workplace.

**Life skills:** I am financially savvy, wisely spending and saving, tracking and organizing records in simple, easy-to-maintain ways. I organize my time and home to efficiently do routine tasks and teach my children how to do them also. I make time for fun and joy and love serving others.

Now you try:

________________________________________

________________________________________

________________________________________

________________________________________

________________________________________

________________________________________

Condense the above sentences into five to seven *total* sentences to define your ideal life.

Your life paragraph:

________________________________________

________________________________________

________________________________________

________________________________________

The finished example might look like this:

"I am a loving, spiritually-centered, happy daughter of God. I enjoy a personal and creative purpose. I connect with family and friends through healthy, positive interactions and communications. I know how to deal with difficult situations and set appropriate

boundaries. I am financially savvy—wisely spending, saving, and tracking and organizing money matters. I balance and organize time and home efficiently and teach my children life skills. I make time for hobbies and fun and delight in serving others."

As a writer, I know that revision is essential to a fine finished product. Have fun and play with it. Give yourself room to revise and redo, making it just right for you.

A life paragraph is powerful. I've been amazed at how it's influenced what I've achieved and become over the years. From it I've created spiritual goals such as attending the temple weekly, physical goals such as losing weight, and life skills goals such as teaching my children homemaking. This paragraph has helped me stay focused on what I want, even when I can't remember what it is!

NOTE: Over the course of the 8-week program, your life paragraph is the one thing that won't change from week to week. Your goal for this particular week is to create a personal life plan. This tool, however, will help in other chapters to guide your remaining goal choices.

## Choose a Weekly Goal

You have finished your life paragraph. Fantastic. Now what? Start your goals! Select simple, focused goals to make it a reality.

For those saying, "What? Goals?," I know this can be a controversial word. But open your mind and put away past associations with New Year's Resolutions (which I no longer set). We all know these don't work, so let them go.

Successful and solid goals are spiritually created first. Following Heavenly Father's pattern, can you think of daily, weekly, monthly, even yearly goals we accomplish both individually and as a family in the Church? Consider daily prayer and scripture study, weekly church attendance and family home evening, monthly temple attendance, and yearly tithing settlement. Through these goals, we consistently stay accountable to ourselves and to the Lord in a healthy, life-changing way.

A note on consistency—you do not need to start with 100 percent achievement. So many of us shoot for the moon and two days later, fail and are shoveling down cake. Instead, be a B+ girl. Shoot for 80 to 85 percent to start, then work toward refining it to 100 percent.

At this point you might think, "There are so many options, I don't know what to choose. More important, which one first?" This is a common problem for women, myself included. I'm a two-fer—I don't want to choose; I want to do both. All the time.

Elder James E. Faust said that as women, we can't do everything beautifully at all times. We can't be 100 percent wife, mother, church worker, career person, and so on all at once. His realistic suggestion, quoting Sarah Davidson, was to "have it sequentially."[5]

Sequentially. Timing. That is the key. Knowing when and how is a discovery process through the Spirit. Heavenly Father knows perfectly what the best timing is for us and our families. Even if blessings—(patriarchal or other)—promise that we will do something, it's not necessarily detailed when and how. We must go to the Lord and ask with an open heart, laying our desires on the altar, earnestly seeking to know His will. He wants only what is best for us, so there is no need to fear. Contrary to popular opinion, great opportunities do come again. And it will be a better opportunity if it creates joy for your family rather than stress.

Initially, the content of the goal is not vital. The key to goal-setting is to *achieve* something weekly. Creating a positive neuro-association —(an intensely happy thought associated with goal-setting)—will get you pumped about future goals. When we reward a new behavior, our nervous system says, "Yeehaw!" (or some equivalent). Consistent conditioning creates what I call "The New Norm"—a new habit that becomes routine.

With your life paragraph in mind, remember successful personal goals are under the umbrella of an overall vision (check), have core values (check), are reasonable, and will include a measurable time frame (double check). They should also make your heart jump—make you feel like, "Wow, I'm baby-stepping in the right direction. Let's get to it."

## Tips to Create Exceptionally Successful Goals

**1. Choose one fabulous goal a week.** Whenever I teach women this concept, inevitably they roll their eyes and say, "I can do more than one goal in a week." Of course they can. For about two weeks. Then the Two-Week Bomb hits, life falls apart, and goals become a dusty paper of the past.

For the eight-week program, each goal will be achieved one time and is unrelated to another goal. Choose projects or things you've put off doing (for example, organize a closet, gather tax records, or set up an exercise and eating program). Or jump-start goals for personal areas (for example, create a scripture study program or read a communication book on connecting with children). Whichever way you choose, set only one solid, tantalizing goal a week and focus on achieving it. Such focus will create immediate change and a positive domino effect in other areas of your life.

Be sure to write your Weekly Goal each week on a new Post-It Page (found in "Back to Basics: More!"). Write it in real-time, using "I will" or "I am." Use specifics that create a commitment but not a burden: "I will work out for twenty minutes Tuesday, Thursday, and Friday at 6:30 a.m." Or, "I am organizing the kitchen counters on Monday and Wednesday while my son naps."

Create a "dangling carrot," the motivating force behind your goal. It should be exciting enough to jump-start a new habit and help you let go of the old one. In a nutshell, use a make-you-salivate Weekly Goal. Do that for eight weeks in a row and you'll be unstoppable.

**2. Have a Plan B.** When it comes to goals, Murphy's Law is in full swing. Create a backup plan to accomplish your desire. For example, if you're working out, choose two realistic times of day. If 6 a.m. finds you snoozing, that's okay; your backup is to exercise at 8 p.m. It doesn't have to be ideal, just flexible. Remember, goals are not sticks to beat yourself with but flexible trampolines to help you soar.

**3. Be accountable to someone.** You know that sweet friend who says you look great when you're sick and doesn't notice when you've gained twenty pounds? Don't choose her. Or the brutally honest friend who makes you tremble when trying on swimsuits because she notices everything? Not that friend either. Find someone who is in between, who helps you see yourself as you are and wants you to succeed.

**4. Reward yourself.** Hands down, this area of the program is the least used. Why? You would think with our perpetual griping (not you, someone else), we would race to reward our efforts. There is nothing sinful about enjoying life in a balanced way. Elder D. Todd Christofferson said that wholesome recreation is the companion of work.[6] You've worked hard, now reward your efforts. Take that hot bubble bath, read that uplifting book, go to breakfast with that dear friend. Make a list of what delights you—even put it in categories of fifteen minutes, thirty minutes, one hour, and so on. You'll have something at your fingertips for gold-sticker time. More reward suggestions are at www.8basics.com.

**5. Use the Post-It Page review.** Not only can you write your Weekly Goal, but you can also complete the review at the end of the week. This helps you evaluate your goal success with three quick questions: what worked, what didn't work, and what to do differently next time. It's not helpful to practice wrong behaviors. This weekly review helps you adjust early on.

Write your Weekly Goal on a Post-It Page and begin achieving it on a Tuesday (because nobody wants to change on a Monday). Accomplish the goal during the week. Then review your success on a Sunday, a day that's hopefully quiet, with time for reflection. If you have children and it's not quiet, make it quiet. Perhaps make a yummy family treat and then invite your husband and children to spearhead the cleanup. Take your quiet time (loosely named) while your family survives twenty fun-filled minutes together.

## Putting It All Together

Wondering how it will look as a finished product? Here's a sample from a woman who has participated in the program:

**1. Emma creates a life paragraph.** "I have a warm, welcoming home, built on the foundation of Christ, filled with love, joy, and laughter; a safe haven for friends, family, and children. I enjoy fulfilling, loving, supportive relationships with my husband and children. I have lifelong, meaningful, and connected friendships. I develop and enjoy new talents and share them in meaningful ways."

She writes her life paragraph on her Post-It Page.

**2. Emma chooses a chapter topic (or life area) and a Weekly Goal.**

*Chapter Topic:* Create Healthy Connections—marriage section

*Weekly Goal:* I will practice effective communication with my husband and show my love for him by listening to him and expressing myself well, using sincere compliments, and greeting him with a hug and kiss.

Emma writes her Weekly Goal on the Post-It Page.

**3. Emma chooses *and uses* a reward.** Buy a new scrapbook binder.

**4. Emma completes a review on the Post-It Page at the end of the week.**

*What worked?* I felt more positive and had a better attitude—expressed my love, spent time with my husband, and felt loved and appreciated back.

*What didn't work?* Sick kids, lost my focus. Didn't use/study the connection principles enough.

*What to do differently?* I need to make some goals that are not so "heavy" emotionally, physically, and so on.

A sample Post-It Page is included to show how Emma's might look.

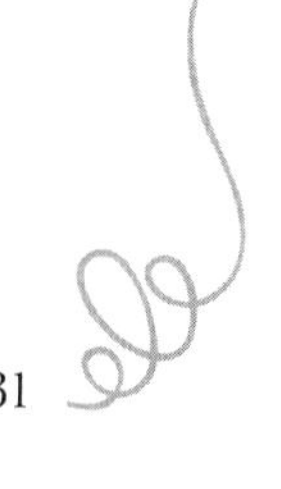

## Post-It Page: Healthy Connections—Marriage

Write your Weekly Goal—include how often, how long, and on what days. Post on your wall. At the end of the week, enjoy a reward and complete the review.

### My Life Paragraph

I have a warm, welcoming home, built on the foundation of Christ, filled with love, joy, and laughter; a safe haven for friends, family, and children. I enjoy fulfilling, loving, supportive relationships with my husband and children. I have lifelong, meaningful, and connected friendships. I develop and enjoy new talents and share them in meaningful ways.

### My Weekly Goal

I will practice effective communication with my husband and show my love for him by listening to him and expressing myself well, using sincere compliments, and greeting him with a hug and kiss.

### My Reward!

I will buy a new scrapbook binder!

### Review:

Consider the past week. Answer the following to create a new goal.

1. **On a scale of 1 to 10 (1=low, 10=high), rate your week's success:** 9
2. **What worked?** I felt more positive and had a better attitude—expressed my love, spent time with my husband and felt loved and appreciated back.
3. **What didn't work?** Sick kids, lost my focus. Didn't use/study the connection principles enough.
4. **What will you do differently in the coming week?** I need to make some goals that are not so "heavy" emotionally, physically, and so on.

**Great job!**

As you can see from Emma's experience, she wrote her life paragraph, chose a life area to focus on (connection), and created a Weekly Goal to improve the relationship. At the week's end, she realized how much it benefited her, what kept her from using communication skills readily, and how to lighten her goal-setting by choosing from a different area next time. Awareness and habits are beginning to change. Give her eight weeks and watch out!

## Wrapping Up

You've discovered what you want, described the details, and created your very own personal plan. Congratulations! Have some chocolate! Continue to tweak and enjoy this plan with the Lord's help. Set *one* solid goal this week—read the suggestions below—and do your best to achieve it. Then reward yourself weekly (or even daily) for a job well done.

### Then What?

Complete the Post-It Page (found in the chapter "Back to Basics: More!" or download it at www.8basics.com). Display it on your wall, in your planner, or on the fridge—wherever you will see it often. Read it, believe it, and ask the Lord to help you achieve it.

Elder Joseph B. Wirthlin stated that it's in seeking the abundant life that we discover our destiny.[7] In getting "back to basics"—spiritually, physically, emotionally, and mentally—you make a masterpiece, a fabulous life that you can't wait to live.

### Caveat: Beware the Two-Week Bomb

Before you set a goal, I want you to envision this possible reality. You've read the chapters, created a vision, and stuck to a goal like skinny jeans for two fabulous weeks. You are woman.

Then life explodes.

You sprain a muscle, your mother-in-law visits unannounced, and worst of all, you've lost the honeymoon excitement of the first two weeks. Now it's just plain work, so forget it and pass the brownies.

Don't panic—this is what I call the "Two-Week Bomb." Somewhere between two and three weeks, life will throw you a curve ball, often many. No one knows why; it's one of those Bermuda Triangle things. Personally, I believe it's good old-fashioned opposition to prevent you from making a life-improving change.

Elder Dallin H. Oaks said that our adversities can be the method of receiving blessings that we couldn't receive any other way.[8]

Whatever adversity you're facing, keep your rhythms. Continue achieving the best you can, completing the Post-It Page with your Weekly Goal and review. Be as consistent as possible. It's a matter of time and consistency, and you will succeed. Remember that if your Weekly Goal ratings are between 8 and 10, that's excellent, so be kind to yourself.

At one point, I did an eating/exercising program, following each step precisely and diligently calculating fat percentages daily. For about two weeks. Then two of my children had birthday parties within days of each other, I got together for a Women's Conference with college friends, and then I had an emergency need for more of my CDs at the BYU Bookstore. For three days, all of those activities meant running crazy and eating on the go. I couldn't bear to weigh myself or take my weekly measurements.

Exasperated, I emailed a friend who had done the program and kept the weight off for sixteen years. Like a soothing mother, she calmed my nerves and recommended I simply continue to do my best and not stress it, and within a few weeks I would lose inches. Staying motivated, by the end of the very next week I had dropped a combined total of five pounds and thirteen all-over inches. Unbeknownst to me, I had still lost weight during the Two-Week Bomb.

Whatever you do, adjust! Rather than force it, work with it. The adjust principle was the beginning of chocolate chip cookies. Back in 1930, as Ruth Wakefield prepared her famous chocolate butter drop cookies one day, the Tollhouse Inn suddenly teemed with customers. With no time to melt the chocolate, she broke it into chunks and threw it in the dough. An after-school staple was born.

When you are midweek and it's obviously a trial, simply adjust your expectations. Reduce or change the goal. For example, if you set the goal to exercise four times a week and suddenly pull a muscle—adjust. Read a motivational book on goal-setting or listen to a fitness book on CD. Switch to a healthy eating goal or nourish your body with more veggies and water. Whatever you do, do something. Move forward, even if it's only millimeters, and this too shall pass.

Like the determined horse stretching for green grass through the fence, push through the Two-Week Bomb, and the other side is truly greener and sweeter. Next year at this same time you will not be stuck in the same place. You will have achieved and become.

## Suggested Weekly Goals to Create a Life Plan:

### *Life Paragraph*

- Complete the brainstorming activity.
- Complete the personal plan.
- Read one chapter in this book that relates to your personal plan (for example, organization or fit and fabulous).

### *Weekly Goals*

- Visit www.8basics.com for more ideas on Rewards. Choose five and post them on your page.
- Do lunch with a friend. Each of you share your personal plan and one way to support one another.
- Write down three things that could keep you from succeeding in your goals. Then add three specific ways to overcome them.

## Notes

Quote at chapter start found in Joseph B. Wirthlin, "The Abundant Life," *Ensign*, May 2006, 99–102.

1. Jeffrey R. Holland and Patricia T. Holland, *On Earth as It Is in Heaven* (Salt Lake City: Deseret Book, 1989), 3.
2. Wirthlin, "Abundant Life," 99–102.
3. Dorothy Draper, quoted in Alexandra Stoddard, *Daring to Be Yourself* (New York: Avon Books, 1990), 26.
4. Wirthlin, "Abundant Life," 99–102.

5. James E. Faust, "A Message to My Granddaughters: Becoming 'Great Women,'" *Ensign*, Sep. 1986, 16.
6. D. Todd Christofferson, "Reflections on a Consecrated Life," *Ensign*, Nov. 2010, 16–19.
7. Wirthlin, "Abundant Life," 99–102.
8. Dallin H. Oaks, "Adversity," *Ensign*, Jul. 1998, 7.

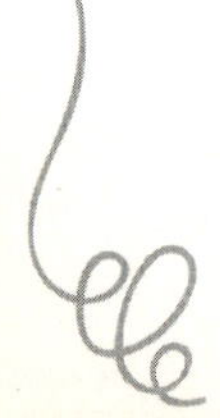

*three*

# discover joy in womanhood

"What do we hear in the gospel which we have received? A voice of gladness!"

D&C 128:19

We are daughters of a loving God. He knows and loves us, as does our Savior Jesus Christ. If the Father and the Son find their greatest joy in our lives—out of the billions of things they could find it in—that's something to feel joyful about.

Yet, in speaking with women over the years, I hear that some feel it's selfish to spend time on oneself, that free time should be spent on serving. Other women hesitate to develop talents, achieve goals, or fulfill dreams, feeling that it isn't allowed. Some women wait for others—a spouse or a good friend—to give them permission to feel joy.

More of these "Joy Drainers" are rooted in worries, distractions, and perceived imperfections. Sister Sheri Dew once said that Satan baits us with temporal pleasures and preoccupations including our bank accounts, wardrobes, and waistlines. He is very aware that where our earthly treasure is, there will our hearts be also.[1]

Each of the reasons for not feeling joy have one thing in common—they can be changed. Add a few "Joy Juicers"—mental and daily shifts—and you *can* feel excited about your life.

## Joy Juicer #1: Be Yourself, Be Your Best Self

We're all unique. Some say weird, others say different, but these words generally mean the same thing: "not like me." We tend to be like seventh-graders: spending our time at recess looking for someone to be with, to say we're not alone, we're not rejected. This concept is what causes grown women to walk to the bathroom together.

Rejoice in your uniqueness, or weirdness, despite how others make you feel. We can celebrate our particular traits and behaviors because the Lord wants and needs diversity. My friend's family loves pickles on their pizza. Another friend enjoys creating food storage recipes with beans. I get giddy in an office supply store. No two women's traits will be alike, so thoroughly enjoy what makes you creatively you.

Sister Patricia T. Holland has said, "The Lord uses us *because* of our unique personalities and differences rather than in spite of them. He needs every one of us, with all our blemishes and weaknesses and limitations."[2]

When we're unhappy, we've likely looked in the wrong direction—sideways rather than upward. In this competitive world, we women can be our own worst enemies. When someone has said something unkind or made you feel insignificant, it doesn't have to rock your world. Respond instead by going to your Father in Heaven to know what He thinks.

Sister Chieko Okazaki shares a profound experience with this very concept. After moving from Hawaii, she planned to teach at an elementary school in Utah. Because it wasn't long after World War II and Sister Okazaki was of Japanese descent, she prepared for possible racism. A few days before school started, the principal told Sister Okazaki that three mothers requested their children be transferred out of her class.

How would you respond to this?

Sister Okazaki didn't take it personally and went about plans for the first day. She shares:

"It could have been a threatening situation. I could have chosen to feel frightened and let the children and parents feel that. Or I could have chosen to be ultra-stern and rigidly professional by way of covering that up. But what I wanted the children to feel was my own joy and excitement."

Rather than hide, she made an exotic-colored dress with a matching flower tucked in her hair. Assembling her first class she could feel their excitement and anticipation.

Later, the principal called Sister Okazaki and mentioned that the three mothers had now asked to have their children reinstated in her class. The principal said, "I told them, 'opportunity knocks only once.'"[3]

Celebrate your unique qualities and let them bless the lives of others.

## On the Flip Side

While I've suggested we rejoice in our uniqueness/weirdness, there is a need to mainstream a bit. A sister may have a diehard testimony of the gospel and a truly obnoxious laugh. Another sister may be a creative genius but cause constant upheaval with last-minute chaos. These traits can be tempered—in fact, the Lord has commanded us to do so. In Ether 12:27, the Lord says, "And if men come unto me I will show unto them their weakness. I give unto men weakness that they may be humble; and my grace is sufficient for all men that humble themselves before me; for if they humble themselves before me, and have faith in me, then will I make weak things become strong unto them."

As we ask Heavenly Father for insight, He'll show us weaknesses that need to be strengthened, and strengths that need to be subdued. That's why callings are vital. In these petri-dish experiences, we learn, share, and grow.

I attended a stake training meeting for ward primary presidencies. All four of the stake presidency leaders stood and, in turn, each shared something about the other that made their presidency a whole. One was a scriptorian and created the spiritual foundation; one liked the froufrou and added fun; one was the umbrella lady who managed the project and process; and the last woman was the finalizer who took care of the finishing touches. Each of these women was blessed with unique talents and innate desires. Yet, it was the sum of the whole that created beauty, order, and a joyful result.

## Back to Basics—Go!

Jot down five things you believe are strengths, talents, or abilities. Then write five things that could be weaknesses. Consider asking

Heavenly Father to help you further develop a strength, add a new one, or work on a weakness (soon-to-be-strength).

| My Fabulous Strengths | My Fabulous Soon-to-Be Strengths |
|---|---|
| 1. | 1. |
| 2. | 2. |
| 3. | 3. |
| 4. | 4. |
| 5. | 5. |

## Joy Juicer #2: Personal Purpose

As women, wives, and mothers, we have plenty of purpose in fulfilling these daily roles. However, by "personal purpose," I mean a purpose that is solely and completely your divine gift. Consider what would acknowledge your creative desires and then find ways to share your gift.

Elder Dieter F. Uchtdorf said that *everyone* can create. As we make unorganized matter into something new, we also change ourselves. And even if we aren't necessarily creative, we ought to remember that we are daughters of a Heavenly Father who is the most creative Being in the universe.[4]

What's your personal purpose? Only you and your Father in Heaven know. Ask Him for what you might not yet see, or start with hobbies and interests that you've let slide. A friend of mine delights in making vintage magnets. Others thrill with quilting, sketching, or gardening. For you it could be singing in the shower or making raisin jewelry. The "what" doesn't matter so much as how it makes you feel—joyful, creative, or inspired.

Whatever you do, choose! Don't worry about not having time, energy, or inclination. Begin today and awaken to a personal expression and contribution that you've been missing.

Elder M. Russell Ballard gave excellent counsel on this concept: "Even as you try to cut out the extra commitments, sisters, find some time for yourself to cultivate your gifts and interests. Pick one or two things that you would like to learn or do that will enrich your life, and make time for them. Water cannot be drawn from an empty well, and if you are not setting aside a little time for what replenishes you, you will have less and less to give to others, even to your children."[5]

That statement is from an Apostle of the Lord. As we follow it, we will feel joy.

## A Word of Caution to This Tale

Having said that (you knew this was coming), I do encourage you to be aware of today's pitfalls. We're to choose, but not at the expense of our family. Just because we love something doesn't mean it becomes our muse. This is not a doctrine meant to suppress—I can personally testify that it is the exact opposite.

For nine years, I ran a part-time business helping women and families improve their lives. From the beginning I promised myself to only spend a couple of hours a day on it because that was generally how long my little ones napped. Through writing books, recording CDs, and having occasional speaking engagements, I choreographed my ability to share concepts similar to the ones in this book. After a few years, I could see that these scripture principles truly helped women and their families. I pleaded with Heavenly Father to help me get this out to more people. And He said, "Not yet."

I continued my part-time schedule—during naps, when children were in school, or in my "free time" (meaning late at night or early in the morning). My business continued to slowly grow—again I asked when I could get this out to more people. And He continued to say, "Wait." At times I felt so frustrated—people's lives could be happier, and yet I wasn't encouraged to do more.

How grateful I am for obedience. How I love Him. Even though I didn't fully understand it, I obeyed. After nine years, I closed the business when it began to consume more than I could effectively give without infringing on my family.

Had I not listened to and followed His promptings, I might have easily been consumed by something—good and wonderful as it was—that could have taken priority over my family during those young, precious years. The business grew, and so did I. No grand shazams, no global confetti, but it was purposeful, enriching, and life-changing.

President Harold B. Lee shared the profound statement that no matter what worthy societies are in the world, a mother's involvement in them would never compensate her for the souls lost in her home while trying to save humanity.[6]

Because I listened to His wisdom—albeit at times reluctantly—today I enjoy thriving, connected family relationships and have no regrets.

## Joy Juicer #3: Have Fun!

That's right, I used the word "fun." About you. When was the last time you had fun? My stake president says that if we're not having fun living the gospel, we're not doing it right.

A few years ago, I carved out some time to go to a bookstore (my place of fun) for about an hour. While exiting the store, I heard the loudspeaker say something like, "Fresh out of the oven, our hot, lemon blueberry scones. Stop by the bakery and try one." They got me. Even though I'm not a scone fan, I salivated. Running to the counter, I nabbed one of those fresh, hot scones and hopped in the car to feast on the drive home. It was out of this world! Melt-in-your-mouth warm goodness with a cold bottle of milk—it was so delicious that I had to call my husband. I told him it was utterly delicious and lamented not buying one for him (as I licked my fingers).

When I talk about having "fun," I mean doing something spontaneous, enjoyable, or wonderful, just for the fun of it. Nothing productive, nothing super-planned, just sheer enjoyment. If you've forgotten how to have fun, watch your children. My son's laugh is so from the gut, high-squeal, can't-breathe hilarious, that wherever I am in the house, I start laughing too.

Years ago I remember my preschool son earned the consequence of washing our tiny bathroom floor. After putting in a load of wash, I came back and saw him swirling the cloth in the bucket, splashing and making airplane noises, and generally having a great time. In typical mom mode, I put my hands on my hips and said sternly, "This isn't playtime—you're to do your consequence." With the words hanging in the air, I started laughing. Totally ridiculous! If he wants to have fun with a consequence, kudos to him.

Have fun. Every single day. Pamper yourself, be gentle with yourself, do something nice for yourself. Life can be hard and appreciation scarce, so do something lovely. What about no chores on Friday? Or stop housekeeping duties after 6 p.m.? Perhaps "Mom's Time" after 9 p.m.? I've used each one, and they have been *fun*.

Obviously I'm not talking uber spa queen, going to an extreme where life becomes all about you. I'm talking about good, old-fashioned, everyday happy things. Someone once suggested to make a list of activities you like doing, and activities you feel good after doing.

For example, "like doing" might be: take a nap, read a book, or go to lunch with a friend. "Feel good after doing," might include working out, baking something your family loves, or cleaning out a closet—initially it may not seem fun, but afterward you feel great. Case in point—have you ever cleaned a closet, and then walked past it again, saying, "Wow, that's a good-looking closet"? That's fun!

### Back to Basics—Go!

List five things you like to do and five things you feel good after doing.

| Like to Do | Feel Good after Doing |
|---|---|
| 1. | 1. |
| 2. | 2. |
| 3. | 3. |
| 4. | 4. |
| 5. | 5. |

## Wrapping Up

Are you excited to find personal purpose? Ready to have some daily fun? Enjoy creating your new week's goal, and remember, *just one*. It will be hard to choose, but there are a few more weeks in the year. Enjoy the paced, consistent joy of achieving in one key area of your life!

## Suggested Weekly Goals for Discovering More Joy in Womanhood

Use one of the choices below or, better yet, create your own!

### *Joy Juicer #1: Be Yourself, Be Your Best Self*

- Complete both Back to Basics—Go! Activities.
- Throughout the week, post a helpful phrase such as "Be Your Bold Self" on your mirror. Repeat daily. Prayerfully choose a weakness and ask how to develop a strength.
- Consider a difficult person who frustrates you. Write down a better response.

### *Joy Juicer #2: Find Personal Purpose*

- Brainstorm creative activities you would like to try. Choose one for this week.
- List three activities a week that are optional—surf the web, watch TV, charter a committee, and so on—and how long you usually spend doing them (be candid!) Choose one to eliminate and use that time toward developing your personal purpose this week.

### *Joy Juicer #3: Have Fun!*

- Brainstorm five things you think would be fun to do. List a few fast fun activities (read a good book for fifteen minutes, lay on the grass for ten minutes, and so on), and then the big fun (run a half-marathon, enter a photography contest, and so on).

## Notes

1. Sheri L. Dew, "We Are Women of God," *Ensign*, Nov. 1999, 97.
2. Patricia T. Holland, "Filling the Measure of Our Creation," in *On Earth as It Is in Heaven* (Salt Lake City: Deseret Book, 1989), 6.

3. Chieko Okazaki, *Lighten Up* (Salt Lake City, Deseret Book, 1993), 49–50.
4. Dieter F. Uchtdorf, "Happiness, Your Heritage," *Ensign*, Nov. 2008, 117–20.
5. M. Russell Ballard, "Daughters of God," *Ensign*, May 2008, 108–10.
6. Harold B. Lee, "Love at Home," chap. 14 in *Teachings of Presidents of the Church: Harold B. Lee* (Salt Lake City: The Church of Jesus Christ of Latter-day Saints, 2000), 129.

# *four*

# feel fit and fabulous

"And the spirit and the body are the soul of man."

D&C 88:15

Maybe you're reading this chapter because you're fed up and want to get in shape. Or maybe it's time to lose the muffin top, or just find a pair of jeans you know will fit. Whatever the specific reason, likely you want to finally feel happy about your body. Yet research shows most women—even women who are at their ideal weight—still won't like what they see. Society, media, friends, even family can contribute to a nagging discontent with our body shape, which creates a distorted body image and can lead to extreme measures for "ideal" beautification.

The fabulous news is that you *can* feel healthy, happy, and fit. Using the principles in this chapter, many women have done just that. They have lost emotional triggers, gained control of their choices, and experienced an awakening of appreciation for their bodies.

Balance, moderation, wisdom: these are simple truths that don't go out of style. If used fully and daily, we'll have and maintain the body and vitality we want.

"Now ye may suppose that this is foolishness in me; but behold I say unto you, that by small and simple things are great things brought to pass; and small means in many instances doth confound the wise." (Alma 37:6).

To become fit and fabulous, inside and out, you can follow three basic principles: eliminate what doesn't work, understand and practice what does work, and fine-tune specific needs for your body. Within these three areas is a lot of information essential to a strong foundation for your future health. *Use the information to choose* one *goal to begin.* Many wonderful, goal-setting weeks are before you in life. Be patient. Start with one and build on that success, incorporating healthy habits as you go.

## Lose Emotional Barnacles

Years ago, President Thomas S. Monson retold a story from a *Church News* article about ships improving their sailing efficiency. He said that as ships travel the oceans, salt-water shellfish called barnacles attach themselves to their hulls. These barnacles "increase the ship's drag, slow its progress, [and] decrease its efficiency." Scraping them off is an expensive and difficult process. But when the captains tie up in Portland, in the fresh waters of the Willamette or Columbia rivers, "the barnacles loosen and fall away, and the ship returns to its task lightened and renewed."[1]

Our bodies can feel lightened and renewed even while traveling through the difficult waters of life. But first, we need to eliminate the barnacles. Let's do this by challenging five false concepts and practices about our bodies with true beliefs and behaviors.

### Body Loathing

God has created, just for you, this beautiful body that functions like no other. People have studied the human body for centuries and are still discovering what it can do. You are its steward. The sooner you nurture and nourish your physical self, the sooner you will see results.

Satan creates discontent. The truth is, he doesn't have a body and wants everyone to "be miserable like unto himself" (2 Nephi 2:27). In the book *No Doubt about It,* Sister Sheri Dew writes that Satan wants us to view our bodies and ourselves as society does, not in the way God does, because Satan tells us that we're not good or smart enough, not thin or cute enough.[2]

God doesn't want a one-size-fits-all body for his family or He would have created that. It's *we* who think it's unattractive. Evaluate fashion and body attitudes through the centuries to track society's fickle taste—one generation's beauty idol is another generation's ugly stick. Today is no different, and it's frightening and unhealthy. One study showed that over the past thirty years, models have become progressively skinnier by almost 15 percent—the same percentage that now denotes anorexia.[3]

**Challenge It.** Overcome body loathing by *expressing daily gratitude* for your seemingly imperfect body. At a friend's suggestion, I started doing a nightly "Body Gratitude Prayer" before sleeping. Beginning at the top of my head, I thanked my Heavenly Father for each body part, what it did for me, and how it was able to carry great stress and yet function so beautifully. Over a few days, then weeks, I noticed key changes. I stopped looking at my belly in the mirror. I smiled more. I now thought and felt, "Wow, I look great at forty-four!"

## Body Worship

On the other end of the spectrum is excessive focus on our bodies, especially in comparison to others. As a young mother, I sat in a Relief Society meeting when a gorgeous lady walked in. Looking like a model with her long beautiful hair and coordinated outfit, she toted a darling baby boy—also fully coordinated—on her slim hip. I disliked her. As I sat wearing my hair clip and tentlike denim jumper, I resolved not to get near her. Over the next few weeks, I could see she was an intelligent person whose comments showed depth and goodness. Wanting to get to know her, I realized that my attitude was prideful and ridiculous. It was all me and my hot button issue—she was slim and put together, and I was not. Repentant, I resolved to introduce myself to this wonderful person and possible friend. The next Sunday, I walked into the meeting only to discover that she and her husband had moved during the week.

Body worship creates competition, which creates enmity between women. Think about the time, energy, and frequency with which you compare your body to someone else's. It can potentially become an idol. The Lord is slowly displaced as number one in daily life through the relentless focus on the physical. Rather than "watch[ing] and pray[ing] continually" (Alma 13:28), you spend the day thinking about how skinny someone else is and how flabby you are, and worrying about what to wear and what you should eat. Consider how often your thoughts stray to body checking instead of living.

**Challenge It.** Let go of the quest for size 2. Just like that. Let. It. Go. Knowledge is power, and knowing your body type helps powerfully release unrealistic expectations. I felt this very thing when reading *Fit and Female* by Geralyn B. Coopersmith.

Coopersmith shares studies by psychologist William Sheldon and French physician Jean Vague to establish six body types (called the "Somatype Theory"), which are a combination of different metabolisms and body shapes:

1. Ectomorphs (high metabolism, naturally thin).
2. Mesomorphs (strong and fit, moderate metabolism, natural muscle tone).
3. Endomorphs (large boned, full-bodied, and slower metabolism).

In addition, the enhancements of "pear" or "apple" are added to complete the body shape:

- Pears are generally more curvy with smaller waists, rounder backsides, and fuller hips/thighs.
- Apples are usually slender with long, lean legs and a general gathering of weight in the stomach and middle area.

To know your possible body type, just combine the two—simple! This prototyping is obviously not set in stone, although I found similar concepts in other cultures that validate the concepts (most notably in Ayurveda, an Eastern Indian view). It is, however, a helpful basic guide to understand your natural body structure.[4]

Once I recognized my shape (Endopear), the concept clicked—this is *my* body shape, so I embraced it! No matter how much I exercised or dieted, my body was not going to be an Ecto of any kind. What a load off. With that freedom, I felt thankful for my curves and a desire to develop my body in the best way for *my* shape. I don't want to be a size 2. I just want to be a sharp-looking, energy-packed, best possible me that I can be.

## Stop Dieting

How old were you when you began your first diet? I often ask this question when I'm presenting, and the results are surprising (so far the youngest has been eight years old). Think about that first diet—did you lose weight? In a healthy way? Do you still practice those principles? I went on my first diet in seventh grade. It was at my mother's suggestion—and the prevailing wisdom of the day—to support my eldest sister with her weight loss. My sisters and I used the Cambridge powder drink for a week. I lost ten pounds. I don't remember what my eldest sister lost, but I do remember her continual battle with mom and weight throughout high school.

Unless you're on doctor's orders, stop dieting—right now. Let go of the nightmare and the false sense of control. Yo-yo dieting is incredibly stressful for the body. It makes lasting weight loss extremely difficult, creates a perceived life threat, and encourages the body to stockpile future calories.

Still think there's the magic diet, lose-one-pound-every-two-days kind of thing that will give lasting results? In the book *Intuitive Eating* by Evelyn Tribole and Elyse Resch, a food-deprivation study was done with thirty healthy men of "superior mental and physical health."[5] In the first three months, the men could eat what they wanted (about 3500 calories a day). But for the next six months, calories were cut to about 1600 per day to mimic chronic dieting.

The results were mind-boggling. Among other things, the study showed that:

- metabolic rates (how efficiently they burned calories) decreased by 40 percent
- the men became obsessed with food—talking incessantly about it, sharing recipes, and so on.
- the men's food behavior became extreme, from ravenous to starvation, and eating styles that included bingeing and bulimia
- personality shifts included irritability, moodiness, and depression
- some men even stole penny candy!

And it didn't stop there. After the study, men found it hard to stop eating and repeatedly splurged on 8,000 to 10,000 calories. It took an average of *five months* to normalize their eating behaviors. Dieting is a losing situation, all right—you lose health, strength, and the ability to lose weight for good.

**Challenge It.** Allow yourself *all* foods. That's right, nothing is taboo. You're a big girl now, and you can choose to eat wisely. One of my fit friends gave me a life-changing axiom—"Everyone can have two bites of anything!" (versus two bites of *everything*). Nothing is forbidden. If you really want to eat something, have it. *But just have two bites.*

As you let go of extreme denial—one dieting woman cried about not having peanut butter—you will reclaim balance and self-control. When you actively choose what to eat, propelled by healthy behaviors, there's no need for a heaping plate of every taste. Natural desires change. You come to crave good food in normal portions (see "The Basic 12" later in the chapter).

## Let Go of Emotional Triggers

Emotional triggers are feelings or experiences—past, present, or anticipated future—that drive us to edible coping mechanisms. These are the things that make us reach for the brownies. The entire pan.

One New Year's Eve in high school, my friend and I didn't have dates. So in a defiant show of we-are-women solidarity, we made other plans. Shortly before meeting for the evening, my friend called and said, "Hey, I got a date. You don't mind, do you?"

What do you think I said? That's right, I said, "No problem" and got in the car, drove to the local Dairy Queen, and downed a hot fudge banana split.

Yeah, that helped.

Being a slave to emotional triggers is no fun. And it doesn't help you move forward in life either. We are mature women now (occasionally) and can handle our feelings more wisely.

What are your emotional triggers? We all feel negative feelings at some point. But an emotional trigger is something that makes you crave or shovel food to cope. Take a minute and circle which emotional trigger(s) you most frequently experience.

| | | | |
|---|---|---|---|
| anger | feel overwhelmed | feel no control | boredom |
| guilt | suppress feelings | feel neglected | rejection |
| being late | make a mistake | humiliated | don't use my voice |
| worry | avoid conflict | hold grudges | my family's choices |
| gossip | people judging me | judge others | others' choices |
| stress | compare myself to others | it looks good | fail at something |

Go back and write the numbers one through five next to your top triggers (1 being the strongest or most frequent, 5 being the least).

**Challenge It.** When you become aware of triggers, you can prepare for them. Consider your top emotional trigger—instead of turning to food, what can you positively do differently? What new *healthy* coping skill can you replace it with? Below are some suggestions.

| | |
|---|---|
| **Use your voice** | "That doesn't work for me." |
| **Set a boundary** | Volunteer for a committee or task for only one hour a week |
| **Journal your feelings** | Keep it private. Delete later what you don't want. |
| **Workout** | Do a FUN workout to eliminate stress |
| **Talk with a friend** | Choose one that listens without judging |
| **Tenderize some meat** | Grab a sirloin and go to it |

For example, in the above situation with my friend, I could have used my voice to set an appropriate boundary (or give a deserving guilt trip) by saying something like, "That's frustrating. We had plans, and now I feel dumped and unimportant."

And then I could have asked if her date had a buddy.

Whichever coping skill you choose, do it a few times or try something new. Allow yourself to experiment with responses that don't include food, and you'll see natural weight loss and increased joy.

## Releasing Negative Social Influences

You are being influenced, every day, about how you should look. And that influence readily transfers to our children, especially the girls. One study showed that about 50 percent of thirteen-year-old girls don't like their appearance, jumping to *80 percent* by the time they are eighteen. And what is the number one graduation gift in many states? Plastic surgery. In one survey of primary-aged children, some girls actually said "they would prefer to live through a nuclear holocaust, lose both of their parents, or get sick with cancer rather than be fat."[6]

And it's not just girls being conditioned to what is pretty, thin, or acceptable. One evening my son and I were at his school square dance for the parents. I stood next to a stick-thin lady with unnaturally proportioned body parts (I will say no more). He turned to me and said, "You're fat mom, but I love you anyway." At that time I was

a size 10. Not only did his allowance suffer, but that night we also had a long, helpful chat about healthy female bodies (and what opinions on mom's body he's allowed to verbalize).

**Challenge It.** We can stop this influence. As women, wives, and mothers, we *must* stop it. Elder Jeffrey R. Holland says, "In terms of preoccupation with self and a fixation on the physical, this is more than social insanity; it is spiritually destructive, and it accounts for much of the unhappiness women, including young women, face in the modern world. And if adults are preoccupied with appearance—tucking and nipping and implanting and remodeling everything that can be remodeled—those pressures and anxieties will certainly seep through to children."[7]

Take a stand. As we stop talking with our friends about "woe is me" and "I wish I were thin," other conversation topics can and will become the new norm. Readily compliment other women—often that's the first one they've heard in weeks. Share your enjoyment of healthy practices and the difference they have made in your life.

A few years ago I wrote a self-development/family column for a popular magazine. Preparing for one issue, I felt impressed to write about unnecessary plastic surgery. My article was candid. With sentences like, "When did *looking* like a mother become akin to leprosy?" I wondered if it would be printed. The courageous editor ran the piece and received a negative response from an advertiser of plastic surgery. However, other women thanked me for the sentiments and felt relieved someone had finally said it.

Now that we've covered some myths and challenged them with truths, have you lost some emotional barnacles? Releasing body loathing, body worship, dieting, emotional triggers, and negative social influences, you've likely lost about ten pounds of stress already. In the next section, we'll gently train your body and soul to embrace enjoyable, healthy habits.

## Intuitive Living

Intuitive living is knowing what your body and soul needs, with the desire and discipline to do it. It's passing up that cupcake—most times—for a better choice *without feeling denied.* My health-focused husband has helped me with this. Instead of a tempting treat, I now see a hydrogenated oil, lard, and white sugar addictive matter with chemicals number 4, 6, and 8, mixed with the same heated enzymes that are used in the construction of plastic.

I don't feel denied at all.

Instead, I wait for a piece of my favorite organic or European chocolate with almonds and enjoy every decadent bite. Changing our daily habits isn't overwhelming, it's more of a conscious process, enjoyably lived. To make good habits simple and intuitive, try the Basic 12.

## The Basic 12

On a typical Sunday morning while getting ready for church, one of our friends suffered a stroke. He had no risk factors. An avid exerciser and healthy eater, he had practiced healthy life principles for many years. Thankfully so, because the doctor needed to look further for the core problem. They found a heart issue, present since birth, of which our friend had been completely unaware. Immediately they performed surgery, potentially saving his life.

What if this man hadn't practiced healthy habits? How likely would it have been for the doctor to say, "Well, eat healthy, start exercising three to five times a week, and come see me in a month or two?" That could have been too late.

Healthy habits eliminate basic issues that make daily life just plain difficult. But what habits are ultimately healthy? With reams of conflicting information, we often have no idea because every food seems to have a downside to it.

I've had this same question. So over the years I've noted a pattern of healthy habits repeated in the most time-tested and reputable programs. I've divided a total of twelve habits into three main categories: eat, exercise, and energize. Simple and true, I call them the Basic 12. Despite popular trends, these core habits bring health and fitness to most people and the ability to maintain them (which is key).

Because your body is unique, you'll have additional tweaks to discover. But to start, the Basic 12 gives your body a solid underpinning on which to build. From there, your body can use its energy and ability to restore itself to further health, often resulting in initial natural weight loss.

(Note: remember, before you begin these habits, please check with your doctor to assess your current physical condition).

| The Basic 12 | | | |
|---|---|---|---|
| **Eat** | | **Exercise** | **Energize** |
| Water instead of soda | Healthy ingredients | 20, 30, or 60 mins. for 3 to 5 times a week | Sleep 7 to 8 hrs. per night |
| 6 small meals a day or 3 meals and 3 snacks | Any meals and snacks before 7 or 8 p.m. | Mix cardio, resistance, and stretch | Pursue personal purpose |
| Fruit and veggies at each meal | Keep a food log for one week | Make it a FUN workout! | Listen to body signals |

Before I briefly explain these twelve habits, you might be thinking, "Is that it? I've done those things and haven't felt healthier or lost weight." But ask yourself two questions: have you truly practiced each of them? And if so, are you still doing them consistently? Remember Naaman. The absurd simplicity of washing himself in the Jordan River seven times seemed fruitless. But he did it. Seven times. (I've often wondered what would have happened if he had stopped at five or six—"See, I told you it wouldn't work.") And he was healed.

These twelve habits are generally self-explanatory, but below is a brief introduction to each of them: the six basics in "Eat," three in "Exercise," and three in "Energize." If you're familiar with these eating habits, feel free to move on to the next section, "Exercise."

## The Basic 12: Eat

**1. Water instead of soda.** Water is a one-stop shop for all things healthy. Water flushes toxins, alleviates constipation, aids in digestion, and helps reverse visual effects of aging. Without adequate daily water, mild dehydration can easily occur, slowing your metabolic rate and burning fewer calories. And drinking a glass of water at night can eliminate those midnight munchies. So, got water?

**2. Six small meals a day or 3 meals and 3 snacks.** Not only does this ease your digestion, but it also encourages your metabolism (the rate at which you burn calories) to be a ready furnace. Smaller meal portions allow your body to more efficiently process food, leading to regular elimination and reducing gas and bloating from overeating.

Within the six meals, try to incorporate the six tastes of sweet, sour, salty, pungent, bitter, and astringent, an Ayurvedic recommendation. As each taste is involved, you will be happily satiated.[8]

**3. Fruit and veggies at each meal.** Choose whatever produce you like, fresh in season, frozen, or canned (in that order). Natural ways of incorporating them work best. Put fruit on your cereal instead of sugar. Use a little fruit in your meal (depending on how it complements the food) *even* if you're planning on dessert. This works! When I included a bit of fruit with my meals, I stopped reaching so much for chocolate and processed treats. The natural sweetness of fruit satiated one of those six tastes and helped me stay balanced.

At first vegetables may seem boring, but trust me—trust me—they will begin to "be delicious to [you]." (Alma 32:28). It's so easy to incorporate them in regular meals or snacks. Try a quality vegetable canned soup (usually zero fat grams)—warm and tasty. Or raw veggies with low-fat ranch dip (mix a seasoning packet in low-fat sour cream)—a little goes an enjoyably long way. And don't start with rutabaga if you can't stand it. Begin with canned sweet corn or add frozen petite green peas. Make zucchini or pumpkin bread or stir pureed veggies into spaghetti sauce—yum. If you must, have a bit of butter (definitely not margarine, which is difficult for your body to process). Or use a natural butter spray—though not fabulous, it will get the ball rolling. Find simple ways to make them an appealing part of your life.

If you're still averse, try a concentrated power-packed vegetable powder from the health food store (I like Garden of Life). Warning: these drinks are extremely bitter, and your taste buds may initially rebel. But the secret is *not* to drink it as is. Mix a quarter or half of a scoop in a chocolate protein drink with frozen banana, and voila, delicious and nutritious.

**4. Healthy ingredients.** When my husband and I were first married, he was a health nut (due to a chronic illness). It drove me crazy. One morning as I commented on his obsessive label-checking, he put my cereal box in front of me and said, "What's in yours?" I remember thinking, "I have no idea." Even though it was a decent choice, I still remember reading out long scientific names, which he then explained in simple terms. And they were not good.

Now who do you think reads labels? In today's stores, healthy foods are everywhere and *can* be convenient—boxed or bagged, in a carton or crate. And we don't have to be diehards about it; this is a process. Add a different grain bread here, eliminate a chemical-laden treat there, and before long, you and your family's natural tastes will return. It will bless your lives in so many ways. A few seconds to check the length of ingredients and what they mean can save you hundreds of dollars at the doctor's office down the road.

**5. Eat any meals/snacks before 7 or 8 p.m.** Allow your digestion at least twelve hours to rest at night before eating again. Your body works hard. Let it rid itself of toxins by finishing your last meal ideally at dinner. Sometimes a later snack may be needed, depending on circumstances. When I had hypoglycemia, I ate a few almonds before bed to stabilize my blood sugar.

**6. Keep a food log for one week.** You're groaning. True, keeping a food log can seem annoying. But if you keep it short and simple, you'll cut right to the meat of what's not working for you. Do it for one week only (download an easy form to put in your planner from www.8basics.com. *Do not change your eating style.* That would defeat the purpose. Simply record what you've eaten (no need to show anyone). At the end of the week, take ten minutes and circle unhealthy eating habits. Note the times of day or events (for example, working late or attending a stressful PTA meeting). Begin to track patterns of when you ate the most, what kinds of food (sugar, carbs, and so on), and how frequently (grab-and-go versus sit down and eat). Use this fabulous information to better plan snacks (10:00 a.m. and the 3:30 dip), avoid sugar traps (the vending machine near the faculty lounge), and deal with boredom (read a good book).

### *Back to Basics—Go!*

Now that you know the Basic 12, let's revisit the chart. Circle what you're *already doing* in daily life. Rate its consistency on a scale of 1–10, 8–10 being the most consistent.

| Eat | | Exercise | Energize |
|---|---|---|---|
| Water instead of soda | Healthy ingredients | 20, 30, or 60 mins. for 3 to 5 times a week | Sleep 7 to 8 hrs. per night |
| 6 small meals a day or 3 meals and 3 snacks | Any meals and snacks before 7 or 8 p.m. | Mix cardio, resistance, and stretch | Pursue personal purpose |
| Fruit and veggies at each meal | Keep a food log for one week | Make it a FUN workout! | Listen to body signals |

If you're doing *any* of it, congratulations! Whether it's a glass of water daily or gardening once a week, it all counts. Most people are doing something healthy, and many people are doing a great deal.

Now that you see what you're doing well, consider what current healthy habit you want to improve or which new habit to implement.

If you choose this category for your *one-time goal*, choose something to help you eliminate a negative habit or begin or increase a healthy one. It could be adding one more fruit and vegetable to your meals five days this week. Or, use two new grains in baking. Or eliminate late-night milk and cookies. Whether you're trying a habit on for size or eliminating one cold turkey, create a goal that will jump-start a healthier you.

For example, one lady I life-coached wanted to make life changes to lower her high stress level. As we discussed several options, I asked if she drank diet caffeinated soda (knowing caffeine would likely worsen her other issues). She paused and hesitantly said yes. I smiled and said, "Well, let's not start with that one. Let's begin with something smaller." To which she replied, "Thank you, or you would find me under the table sucking my thumb."

Instead, I asked her to drink one glass of water before drinking any soda—a glass for a glass. This was doable. It started a healthy habit (drinking water) so she could eventually eliminate the negative habit (drinking soda and caffeine).

## The Basic 12: Exercise

You're likely already exercising in some form without realizing it. In an average week, you might have walked a little, played a sport with your children or grandchildren, and done a bit of yard work or snow removal. Congratulate yourself on these successes; it all helps!

Now add FUN workouts, meaning "For Ur Nurture." When we stop driving our bodies so hard to lose weight and use nurturing workouts, we suddenly find natural movement enjoyable. *And we lose weight.*

To create enjoyable and effective workouts, evenly rotate within a week some cardio (known as aerobic), resistance (strength or muscle training), and stretching (calisthenics, Pilates, and so on).

Choose workouts that are enjoyable for a beneficial length of time (depending on if you're just starting, work out occasionally, or are a regular gym girl). Workouts can include gardening, cleaning, even bowling, all burning between 170 and 239 calories per hour. Get with a friend or group if you're a social exerciser, or buy Latin dance DVDs if you're more individual. Make it FUN, and you will be consistent. When my daughter went to kindergarten, I was able for the first time to conveniently drive to an exercise class, which happened to be Zumba. I loved it! So much that for months I went three mornings a week, without fail. When you love it, you'll make time for it.

To begin FUN workouts, enjoy any movement for any length of time. In her book *The Confident You,* Barbara Barrington Jones tells of one woman who began exercising by walking to her mailbox and back. After a while, she increased the distance and then the time to forty-five minutes, six days a week. She lost over one hundred pounds.[9] Begin where you are, for fun, then work up to twenty, thirty, and sixty minutes down the road. If you're running late, break up the workout into two sessions (briskly walk for a doable fifteen minutes at lunchtime and midafternoon).

For your one-week goal, and if you're new to exercise, take it slow. Perhaps do two days cardio (brisk walk or light aerobics), one or two days light resistance (low reps of lunges or core training), and three days off alternated in between. Rest is crucial to rebuilding muscle and losing weight, so don't think days off are unproductive. Start slow, build solid, and maintain with joy.

If you're still not convinced FUN workouts are for you, hear this: exercise creates after-burn, meaning you continue to burn more calories for anywhere from fifteen minutes to forty-eight hours. And it releases the same mood-boosting endorphins (brain chemicals) and similar feelings you receive after *eating chocolate.*[10] Zumba anyone?

***Back to Basics—Go!***

To be most effective, create a workout plan from which you can choose programs that you love to do. Write under each column a workout that you *already enjoy* (for example, cardio—walking; resistance—lunges; stretching—Pilates). *Choose one workout from each column during the week.* Add new ones or rotate familiar favorites. I still use exercise DVDs and tapes from ten to twenty years ago because they're fun and still get results.

## My FUN Workouts

| Cardio | Resistance | Stretching |
| --- | --- | --- |
| | | |
| | | |
| | | |

If you're not sure which workouts are best for you, go online, ask your workout friends, or use Ms. Coopersmith's suggested exercises in her book, *Fit and Female,* for the Endo, Ecto, or Meso body types. She has detailed and excellent workouts for each unique body type. And remember to mix it up. If you've exercised regularly and are not seeing results, it's possible that you're not balanced between cardio, resistance, and stretching.

## The Basic 12: Energize

Do you need more sleep? Do you want more purpose and motivation in your life? Energize is the most overlooked category of the three. Because we think it's fluffy. Or we don't have time. Or it's not convenient. But including and valuing energizing means increased health, better body functions, and natural weight loss. Let's look at three types of energizing methods that work: rest, personal purpose, and listening to your body.

**1. Rest.** When I experienced adrenal fatigue, I had been working out six days a week, forty-five to sixty minutes a session. Finally thrilled to be consistent, I now had to force myself *not* to exercise in order to heal (the irony of it all). Working out wasn't helping my exhausted body. However, as I enjoyed consistent, quality rest, my energy improved to neutral, then increased. Steadily. So have faith in rest. Sleep first, get back to neutral, *then* gently increase your workout time for optimum wellness.

**2. Personal purpose.** Go back to your life paragraph—what do you love to do, experience, or dream about? Think about your hobbies, passions, and pursuits that stay locked in the closet because of zero time or energy. Add spice to your life with something quick and fun (read a book, take a hot bubble bath) or with more purposeful pursuits (teach a cake decorating class or attend one). Start focusing energy on something joyful, even creative, and you will get a charge of positive attitude and motivation for your life.

Review Elder M. Russell Ballard's counsel in chapter three to make time for something enjoyable and write it down. This will help you remember what you like to do and feel good after doing. Choose one and enjoy!

**3. Listen to your body.** Begin listening to your body by noting its particular signals—what they are and what they mean.

At one point in my life, I gained and lost twenty to thirty pounds several times, within a few years, all while practicing the *same* healthy habits. I couldn't understand it. I ate between 1800 to 2000 calories a day and exercised five to six days a week for forty-five to sixty minutes, mixing cardio and weights. At one point, I gained twenty pounds in six months! Desperate, I did more (which created adrenal fatigue), tried unusual remedies (honey and cinnamon at night *does not* make you lose weight—I gained another five pounds), and alternative methods (acupuncture, ginger tea in the mornings, and liver cleanses).

After more than a year of experimentation, guess what I found? The problem was not my body; it was me. The tried and true did work—I simply hadn't listened to my body signals. When I tuned in, my body responded. Paying attention to sudden ringing ears, extreme thirst, and exhaustion, I recognized signs of adrenal fatigue. Instead of exercising more, I exercised less, adding helpful natural supplements to nourish my depleted glands. Symptoms of shaking hands and bursts of ravenous hunger clued me in to possible hypoglycemia. Rather than eat less, I ate about 2,000 calories of healthy foods in frequent intervals throughout the day. The symptoms stopped. In each case, my body was clearly telling me something. I only had to listen closely and decipher the message.

Through this and other experiences, I finally stopped focusing on pounds, felt gratitude for my beautiful and divine physical gift, healed illnesses that reduced my quality of life, and ultimately lost weight and kept it off.

## Fine-Tuning Your Body

Let's say you're living pretty healthy right now. You've eliminated the emotional drag and practiced the Basic 12, but for some reason, your body won't lose weight. Or, you're experiencing some unusual body signals and aren't sure what they mean.

It's very possible that your hormones are out of balance.

Years ago, between babies (and after having several), my body was out of whack. I felt cold all the time, couldn't lose weight with low-calorie meals, and had what my family affectionately termed "wench episodes." My nails were brittle, my energy and love for life were at an all-time low, I had hot flashes, and I couldn't sleep at night.

Finally, I discovered bioidentical hormones. Within days of using them, my wench episodes were gone. Within a month, I'd lost eight pounds, and within three months, I felt almost back to normal.

Bioidentical hormones use soy to create natural female hormones that very ably match a woman's body (note: this is *not* the grocery shelf soy). Bioidentical hormones differ from synthetic hormones because they are made from natural substances that your body can generally receive and use without a negative response. Synthetic hormones have been found to cause a variety of problems. A government-sponsored study called the Women's Health Initiative was done in 2002 to *refute* negative associations between synthetic hormones and cancer. It was supposed to last over eight years, but the study was stopped after just over five years because the risk outweighed the benefits. The synthetic hormones actually *increased the risk* of breast cancer, stroke, heart disease, lung blood clots, and other health issues by 26 to 2,100 percent.[11]

My and other women's experiences have been life-changing. If you've experienced similar hormone symptoms, please take the time to visit a doctor *experienced and well-researched* in natural bioidentical hormones. Check his or her background, information, and views on the subject. It's worth your health.

## Wrapping Up

Are you excited to let go of negative habits and embrace a healthier lifestyle? You know how. You've learned to stop body loathing, body worship, dieting, emotional triggers, and society's influence. Using the Basic 12—at an enjoyable pace—you know how to implement healthy habits.

Now, choose your Weekly Goal, in one area (Lose Emotional Barnacles; Intuitive Living—Eat, Exercise, or Energize; or Fine Tuning), and enjoy stepping on the healthy road to fit and fabulous, both body and soul.

Note: for more ideas, check out the "Get Fit & Fabulous" CD, available at www.8basics.com, or the bonus tips below to jump-start your one-time goals.

### Bonus Tips

Choose one of these tips as a one-time goal that can also become a lifestyle habit. I now use and enjoy all of them with great results.

**1. Save and Spend.** Each day you can know how many calories are needed to nourish your body (calculate daily needed calorie and fat grams in the "Back to Basics: More!" chapter at the back of the book).

Let's say you can play around with about 2200 to 2500 calories a day, and about 40 to 60 fat grams. With the "save and spend" concept, choose to *save* fat or calories on some meals (hold the cheese and ham on my omelet) to *spend* them at another meal (dessert for date night). Saving is easy and fun!

Perhaps one meal you feel like a ham sandwich, chips, and brownie sundae. To save and spend, use turkey instead of ham, wheat bread instead of white, add lots of fresh sandwich veggies, mustard, and low-fat mayo (not fat-free), baked chips instead of regular, with carrots and low-fat ranch dip, then finish up with a low-fat chocolate truffle bar for dessert.

The first option adds up to 1,340 calories and 74.5 fat grams. My save and spend option gives me 706 calories with only 15.5 fat grams. Delicious and filling, I just saved over 600 calories and almost 60 fat grams in a single meal.

**2. Half your portion.** You've heard it, but this time, try it! At a restaurant, immediately scoot half the portion to the side (or even better, in a box), *without feeling denied.* How? Know that you're saving calories for dessert that night, and the remaining portion for lunch the next day—what could be better? Use smaller plates for dinner—instead of large cereal bowls, use a glass dessert cup. It's a proper portion and, after adding some fruit and nuts, completely satisfying. This works! Reducing calorie intake by 100 to 300 calories a day could mean losing 10 to 30 pounds by next year—enjoyably and naturally.

**3. Look your best.** Stand up straight, like your mother said, and you'll look slimmer and more confident. Change out the old college hairdo for a flattering cut with highlights—and maintain it. You likely have clothes that you never wear, want to wear but won't, and likely shouldn't wear (think anything with large polka dots). Whiten your teeth. Pluck your eyebrows. At least use lipstick or eye pencil, even when you don't feel like it. Dress for the day, if only for errands or playdates. Show self-respect in how you dress, speak, and behave.

Try one bonus tip for your Weekly Goal. Each is a great way to jump-start self-confidence, better health, and successful weight loss.

## Suggested Weekly Goals for Feel Fit and Fabulous

### *Lose Emotional Barnacles*

- Before going to sleep, express gratitude for your body, starting from your head down to your toes.
- Determine your body type and list all of the positive traits.
- Identify an emotional trigger and choose a healthy coping skill to use this week.

## Suggested Weekly Goals, continued

### *The Basic 12*

- Choose one negative healthy habit and replace it with a positive healthy habit from the Basic 12.
- Complete the FUN Workout chart and choose one to begin this week.
- Decide one way you can relax and the time you can do it and then begin this week.
- Research bioidentical hormones and see if they are right for you.
- Use one of the bonus tips to jump-start healthy change this week.

## Notes

1. Thomas S. Monson, "Your Eternal Voyage," *Ensign*, May 2000, 41.
2. Sheri L. Dew, *No Doubt about It* (Salt Lake City: Deseret Book, 2001), 133.
3. Geralyn B. Coopersmith, *Fit and Female* (Hoboken, NJ: Wiley, 2006), 14–15.
4. Coopersmith, *Fit and Female*, 39–41.
5. Tribole and Resch, *Intuitive Eating* (New York: St. Martin's, 1995), 59–60.
6. Coopersmith, *Fit and Female*, 17.
7. Jeffrey R. Holland, "To Young Women," *Ensign*, Oct. 2005, 28–30.
8. Linda Banchek, *Cooking for Life* (Fairfield, IA: Orchids and Herbs Press, 1989), 2–3.
9. Barbara Barrington Jones, *The Confident You* (Salt Lake City: Deseret Book, 1992), 8.
10. Coopersmith, *Fit and Female*, 60.
11. Suzanne Somers, *Ageless* (New York: Crown Publishers, 2006), 21.

*five*

# find balance in motherhood

"There is *no* one perfect way to be a good mother."

Elder M. Russell Ballard

The story is told of a keeper of a town spring. He worked hard to maintain the water's purity and freshness that filtered into the town shops, homes, farm fields, and wells. But one year the town budget cuts extended to the keeper, with the idea that he wasn't necessary after all. In a short time, the water became polluted, the crops failed, and the animals died. The town voted to reinstate the keeper, who brought the spring back to its former life-giving status.

That's motherhood. We are the keeper of the springs. Sometimes society, media, or even those close to us don't value the day-in-day-out of motherhood that is so vital to the Lord's work. But try to shortchange it, and the result isn't pretty. Despite the lack of accolades, rewards, or monetary compensation, mothers have been given a holy calling and pivotal opportunity—one that will impact generations to come.

Knowing both how important motherhood is and how little valued it can be, how do we balance this overwhelming but wonderful responsibility? Given the go-go of scripture study, scouting activities, school, lessons, listening, dinner—and that's just getting started—how can we not only balance but also more fully enjoy motherhood?

## Appreciate Your Unique Family

Just as there are no perfect mothers, neither are there perfect families. Elder Ballard finished the statement at the beginning of this chapter with this: "Each situation is unique. Each mother has different challenges, different skills and abilities, and certainly different children. The choice is . . . unique for each mother and each family. . . . What matters is that a mother loves her children deeply and, in keeping with the devotion she has for God and her husband, prioritizes them above all else."[1]

What a relief that, above all, we are to love and prioritize our children. As we face our challenges, there is no need to worry what others think or to compare our unique family to someone else's. At a conference several years ago, I asked women to share what gave them joy. Many shared typical experiences—births, weddings, children serving missions or attending college, and so on. After class, two women approached me and hesitantly told me their joys: one said it was knowing where her son was at night; the other said it was when she kissed her son's head, and it didn't smell like marijuana. I embraced these women, expressing my wish that they had shared these thoughts in class. How many other women in that room could have related to atypical "joyful" experiences?

We can embrace our family reality and then work toward the ideal for our situation—married or divorced, widowed or remarried. Using inspired counsel, we have the basic building blocks of a strong family fortress.

In 1999, the First Presidency issued a letter to parents encouraging them "to devote their best efforts to the teaching and rearing of their children in gospel principles which will keep them close to the Church. . . . We counsel parents and children to give highest priority to family prayer, family home evening, gospel study and instruction, and wholesome family activities. However worthy and appropriate other demands or activities may be, they must not be permitted to displace the divinely-appointed duties that only parents and families can adequately perform."[2]

For our purposes, we'll condense this counsel to four basic things: family home evening, family prayer, family scripture study, and wholesome recreation. (That is, fun!)

Let's consider ways to practice these more fully—and enjoyably—in daily family life. As in previous chapters, there will be a good amount of information. Please pick and choose sections that appeal and apply to your particular family's needs.

## Create Vital Family Traditions

Sister Cheryl C. Lant encourages us to consider our traditions—if they are focused on the material or the eternal. If we proactively create righteous traditions rather than let life happen to us, it will be easier for our children to follow prophetic counsel.[3]

Consider the traditions that will best benefit your family. Which are most essential to incorporate right now? I think about the mothers of Helaman's stripling warriors and the time, patience, and energy they must have put into those boys aside from helping with their daily must-dos (hunt beasts, clean their tents, pick up their animal hides). These mothers obviously spent time on daily necessities but apparently focused their best energy on spiritual matters. How do we know? From everything their sons were taught, they remembered the spiritual and obeyed. And it saved their lives.

As you choose how to implement the principles from the First Presidency message, what kinds of new traditions will you create? Perhaps family scripture study is around the table, on grandma's antique brass bed, or in the car on the way to school. Maybe family home evening is cotaught weekly by a child with a parent, or includes a predictable primary song. Sister Beck shared in a Worldwide Training Meeting that her family sang "Love at Home" at every family home evening for years. When she asked her father why they had to keep singing the same song, he told her, "When you have learned lesson one . . ."

Create traditions of these four building blocks—family home evening, scripture study, prayer, and fun—with your family's input. Involve them, listen to them, and help them enjoy it.

Let's look at ways to implement just two of the building blocks—prayer and scripture study. As we do, keep in mind a wonderful insight from Sister Chieko Okazaki in *Lighten Up*. "In principles, great clarity. In practices, great charity."[4] Meaning, rules are not tight constraints to awkwardly bind us—they are wise parameters to allow creative application for our needs. Do what works best for you and your family, and you'll have the tradition *and* the joy.

**Prayer.** When my children run out the door, saying, "No time for prayer," they are gently (mostly) guided back with, "There is always time for prayer." Find the way to make it work. Perhaps your family can gather at 5 a.m. and kneel in joyous silence. In our home, not a chance. But we do have several prayers throughout the morning—before school with the boys and my husband, and later with the girls and myself. We've had prayer by phone when my husband traveled, and in the car after returning home from a late family activity. Be flexible, switch it up, but just do it, every day, twice a day, to start and end it in unity.

**Scriptures.** At some stages of family life, nightly reading thirty minutes of straight text would put both parents and children over the edge. So have fun with this! Mix it up and try something new. Scripture charades are perfect for younger children, especially after an exhausting day. While my husband and I lie on the couch in a stupor, the children knock themselves out acting out scripture people, items, or stories. Share excerpts from the *New Era*, the *Friend*, or conference talks (special stories are now conveniently referenced at the back of the conference report). Have a testimony sharing night or read from a parents' scripture or gratitude journal.

Years ago, I attended a Relief Society meeting where a wonderfully overzealous woman had typed pages upon pages of scripture. We cut them into strips and placed them in a jar. Heaven! We still use these "Scripture Strips" in the morning (for more information, go to www.8basics.com). We choose one, read it, and ask what it means (and they say daily, "Jesus loves us," so I have to get them to actually think about it).

Perhaps listen to scriptures on tape while your little ones draw a "scripture picture" of what they're hearing. Listen to a conference CD during a teenager's carpool or watch an animated scripture movie on Sunday and discuss it afterward.

Keep it flexible and creative. For a few months, I drove my eleven-year-old to school in the mornings. As we drove, I asked him to read the scriptures. He said he couldn't read because it made him carsick. This is the same child that had been glued to a popular young adult book for an hour while riding in the family car, squinting with just a dim overhead light.

Carsick my eye.

What he really wanted to talk about was a popular video game. So I told him we'd compromise—he could share with me how the video game was like the gospel. And he did! He said, "The blue square is like repentance because it's a plus three, and the red square is sin because it's a minus seven," and so on. It was great! Maybe we served "God and mammon," but he got his daily scripture dose and still remembers it today.

Whatever traditions you choose, make family home evening, prayer, scripture study, and fun a part of your family's life. Simply try it, use it, do it, and enjoy it! We can find what works best for our particular family to draw closer to the Savior.

## Raise Your Children as Future Adults

When my son was seven, he wanted a Lego set. "It's only forty-four dollars, Mom," he said. I smiled and replied with, "How do you want to earn that money, sweetie?" A short while later, I came downstairs to the kitchen and saw a marvelous work and a wonder—he had upended the kitchen stools on top of the table and was mopping the kitchen floor. I was dumbfounded. His chores up to that point had been matching socks and cleaning his room. Gone were those days.

We can allow our children to step up. In fact, we need to. If we are to develop future stellar adults, we must give them opportunities to practice.

Consider your daily routines, errands, and must-do lists. How can your children begin to do some of them—especially those abilities they will use in the future? Doing laundry, cleaning rooms, using a budget, cooking dinner—these are all life skills each child needs to progressively learn. Involve your children, teach them how, and give them opportunities to do it themselves.

An obvious caveat here: we are not dumping chores on our children in the name of "teaching" and going off to the spa. I'm talking about teaching, training, and turning over family jobs that will prepare them for a productive life.

In *All Rain, No Mud*, Sister Sharon Larsen tells about when her sister, Shirley, had a dryer in need of repair. Her son—fascinated by machines—volunteered to do it. She debated, as his "fixing" attempts had not always gone well, but she took a deep breath and let him try. Sister Larsen said, "When [Shirley] finally heard the hum of the dryer, she realized that her 'witness after the trial of her faith' had arrived. Lincoln became the repairman. Anything that needed repairing, Lincoln was on duty, and he knew it."[5]

How do you think this affected Lincoln's self-confidence and his future abilities as a husband?

Daily teaching moments abound. My older boys have hung pictures, fixed the vacuum cleaner, and assembled a trampoline. My younger girls have completed three days' worth of laundry, weeded the yard, and cooked dinner (not on the same day and not without trauma). Yes, the pictures might be crooked or the dinner unrecognizable, but the essential principle is to give them the opportunity, early and repeatedly. My children start folding towels at about age three—they look like bowling balls. But by the time they are five (or fourteen), the towels are stacked as flat as pancakes. Parenting is a process—allow your children opportunities to grow.

And this suggestion isn't just for temporal tasks. You and your husband can delegate spiritual practices in appropriate ways so that children know how. They can take turns teaching family home evening—which also counts for Duty to God, Faith in God, and likely a badge for something or other. Have them prepare a devotional or lead out a spiritual discussion at the dinner table. We can stop being controlling and let them develop life skills, bringing lifelong and eternal dividends.

And if you're feeling badly that you haven't implemented some of these principles, don't stress! Simply start something today. At times I've worried about the impact on my children from not having ideally applied a principle. However, I've discovered a few things. First of all, that's part of motherhood. Second, I've actually done more than I thought. And lastly, when newly applied, my children are generally good about accepting a change (I ignore rolling of eyes). Over time what was new becomes routine.

## Require Respect

My children used to think I was like the Energizer bunny—I could keep going, and going, and going . . . It was my fault because I proved it daily by being available for everyone and everything. This was unwise. Through time and experience, I came to realize that not

only was I hurting my own health and self-esteem, but I was also setting my children up with expectations and behaviors that could negatively impact them in future relationships.

I'm not suggesting that self-sacrifice is a bad thing—motherhood is all about that. I am saying that the Savior was selfless, yet He still created clear boundaries. Although He spent most of His time with others, He still went "up into a mountain [to be] apart"—to be alone (Matthew 14:23). His time was also appropriately divided among people—mostly the multitudes, at times only His Apostles, and at other times a few close friends such as Mary, Martha, and Lazarus. Though He constantly served, the Savior clearly knew His identity, role, and the one "needful" thing at any given time (Luke 10:42).

If you're feeling off-balance, you can change it. We are the moms, and we set the tone. A mother should be prized, revered, and most certainly appreciated. If that's not happening in your home, set a new and healthy parameter. Once you set the example, their behaviors will follow—not without time, struggle, and constant repetition. But it will change because you have.

My children know that if they complain about dinner, they receive a second helping. Perhaps as an outgrowth, they also say thank you at just about every meal. In fact, this practice hit such an annoying pitch—"Mom, you're the best cooker ever" and "Mom, you should open a restaurant"—that I finally put the kibosh on schmoozing mom. But they got the concept—if I've taken time to prepare it, they can express gratitude for receiving it. One of our sons daily thanks Heavenly Father for "great parents"—sure, he knows who pays his babysitting money, but it works for me. If my daughter forgets a school paper, she already knows that mom is not the Last-Minute Limo Driver—she will either not call or trade the trip for a chore.

If you're not receiving respect—for yourself or what you do in the home—maybe it's time to set a new boundary. When I experienced adrenal fatigue a few years ago, I felt constantly tired, had chills and ringing ears, and was left without motivation or energy for life. As I considered what to do (fly to Hawaii for a month?), I was struck with the realization to implement what had worked before. It was clear that over time, our family had strayed from initially structured and successful routines to doing just the bare minimum.

So I reinstated three things. First, the older children became mentors again to the younger ones—helping with homework, dressing for Sunday, and so on—which conserved energy and reduced nagging. Second, I chose chore supervisors. On cleaning day, one of the older children was responsible to check each person's jobs and sign off on its completion.

Third, I carved out daily down time. As I considered the children's schedule, I noted that after everyone had returned from school, snacked, and relayed their day to me, there was free time for about forty-five minutes before beginning chores and dinner. I put a sign on my bedroom door—"Do Not Disturb. Mama Is Resting"—with a warning that it would not be opened for anything but blood or broken bones (and those were negotiable).

For the first few days, there was the usual banging on the door for really urgent questions ("Where is my toy pony?") and general wailing and gnashing of teeth. But miraculously, after a few days they got the concept, and there was peace in the land. I rested for forty-five minutes and was able to finish the evening hours with enthusiasm.

Think about what appropriate ways your family could show more respect for you and motherhood. Choose one and make it your new mantra.

## For Your Particular Stage of Life

Because I'm addressing mothers in various stages of motherhood, this last section is divided into more specific helps for young mothers, mothers of teens, and empty nesters. Feel free to skip to the title that best matches your particular situation or go right to "Wrapping Up."

### Young Mothers

In this stage, the days can often be long and tedious, full of repetitive tasks and teaching. I hear what the President of the United States does on a daily basis, and I think, *snore*. Come to my house with six children—teenagers to a kindergartner—and just try to tell me your troubles.

Elder M. Russell Ballard emphasized that motherhood's joys come in moments. Although there will be difficult times, even amid the challenges there are beautiful pockets of happiness.[6]

How do you merge the privilege and joy of rearing divine spirits

sent from God, and the day-to-day reality of spooning pureed peas into an unwilling mouth?

**A suggestion.** Remind yourself daily that what you do is sacred. Remember that motherhood is priceless, especially on days that seem endless and eternal (usually that's when a sweet older sister says, "Enjoy these years—they're the best of your life" and you sort of feel like punching her in the nose).

Years ago, I was assigned to be the concluding speaker at a Relief Society meeting. Arriving before my scheduled time, I stepped unnoticed into the back of the room while another speaker finished. Before me sat row upon row of young mothers, many of them rocking a baby on their shoulder or entertaining a toddler on their laps. Immediately and fully, I felt a sacred, tangible Spirit in that room. The feeling overwhelmed me to tears. And, simultaneously, I sensed that these good women did not comprehend the holiness of what was happening—they were just doing what moms do.

Through the sleep-deprived haze, you can create more moments of joy and gratitude—many of them. Ask Him how to do it. Let Him carry the load for you. Pray to find out what you most need, and He will tell you.

A wonderful way to appreciate this adventurous stage of life is to take regular time off. When I was in the thick of four children—the oldest being six—I felt inspired to take one night out a week for myself. I spent two to three hours every Wednesday night at a local bookstore. Curled up in a chair, I could enjoy a book and a slice of cheesecake—uninterrupted. When I returned, I was thrilled to see my children, did not care about the state of the house (good thing), and gave my husband an appreciative smooch. Along with spiritual habits, this practice saved my sanity during those difficult years.

Time off may mean a "No Chores" day or joining a Saturday morning running group. As mentioned in a previous chapter, Elder M. Russell Ballard has counseled women to choose something they love to do and then make time to do it. And he's further invited our husbands to give us the day off once in a while and take over household duties.[7]

Use this wise counsel. Go to the temple, take a craft class, enjoy a hike in nature—you can do this! Trade with a friend, barter with a neighbor, or take turns with your husband, but make it happen. Find what connects the woman part of you to the mother part of you to keep rejuvenated and continue enjoying your children. Do what's vital to care for the keeper of the spring.

## Mothers of Teens

The teenage years can be the ultimate adventure. Sister Larsen tells this experience in *All Rain, No Mud*:

> One night our boy was angry with us and used model airplane glue to seal my husband, Ralph, and me in our upstairs bedroom. . . . While I was thinking of tying bed sheets together, . . . Ralph was eyeing our clothes chute. . . . Do you remember the story of Winnie the Pooh visiting Rabbit in his hole and . . . he got stuck? . . . That was Ralph, trying to wriggle his body through the clothes chute to get into the hall. He finally made it. We were no longer held captive, but our hearts were sad.[8]

Teen times can be turbulent. But they can also be some of the best and most memorable bonding experiences with your son or daughter. Every day, these young men and women are defining themselves, testing what you've told them, and seeing the world and situations with their own eyes. They're thinking (occasionally), feeling (underline this for girls), becoming aware of problems (not about themselves, just about everyone else), and devising solutions (albeit creative ones).

**A suggestion (or two).** At this stage, it's listen, love, set clear boundaries together, and give them opportunities for spiritual experiences. Ask their opinion and take their suggestions as often as you can. They will more openly respect you as you respect them. Don't let eye rolling stop you from doing what is best for them. Elder Robert D. Hales said that often we are afraid to counsel our children for fear of offending them. But instead, we are to define clear boundaries and follow through.[9] A friend of mine practices the adage, "Trust, but verify."

In the process, however, we can lighten up a bit about things that aren't vital. My husband likes to remind me, "Is this the hill you want to die on?"—meaning, pick your battles. Remember you're on the same team, particularly when they don't even seem to play the same sport.

Love them when they're unlovable, even when you feel nothing is getting through. President Harold B. Lee said not to give up on teenagers in their potentially annoying states of egotism and irresponsibility, or when they are apparently not listening. At some point, yours may be the book they take off the shelf and read in their distress.[10]

Do what you can; love them in the way they need to be loved. Shower them with specific praise and positive affection. Discover their love language—how they most feel loved. Most of my teenagers' love languages are verbal and touch—it's exhausting! But it becomes a great gift to me as it is returned—asking about my day and giving me foot rubs. I say, "Train up a child in the way he should go, and hopefully he won't have amnesia," or words to that effect.

Be creative, not reactive, and most importantly, have fun with them. One day my verbose son (doesn't matter which, they all talk a lot) was detailing his latest hobby with great passion and a technical language that was completely lost on me. After about fifteen minutes, I couldn't take it any longer. I told him I had to use the restroom and started walking toward it. He turned in astonishment and said, "I don't care!" and kept talking to me through the closed door. So I did what any mature mother would do. Sticking my fingers in my ear, I hollered through the door, "LA LA LA LA LA LA!"

Lastly, give them opportunities for spiritual experiences. Trying to be the good parents, we can unwittingly limit our children's spiritual experiences by doing it for them. Then we wonder why they don't have a strong testimony. In keeping with your children's understanding, give them opportunities to pray about problems and consider possible solutions. Share scriptures with them and include personal experiences. A good part of the time, they will stare at you like you're growing gills, but that's okay. Just keep at it and create a new tradition of how you handle difficult situations.

Our son was planning to attend a physically demanding, week-long campout set in a canyon. The boys would be hiking each day, rappelling off one-hundred-foot cliffs, and for three days solid be without any contact with the outside world. Though we wanted him to share in that bonding experience, our son had been fighting an upper respiratory infection. The week before he was to go, the symptoms still lingered. The doctor said it was best if he was 100 percent better but thought it likely everything would be fine and left the decision to us. We talked with our son, shared our concerns, and asked for his opinion and for all of us to pray about it. Our son prayed and then came to us and said that he felt he shouldn't go. We agreed. He stayed home, and within a few days, his condition significantly worsened. We were grateful he was at home to receive the medical attention he needed.

Not every situation will be like this. Sometimes we've asked this same son to pray about something (for example, difficult, boring, strenuous tasks), and he has received a different answer than us. That's a great moment to discuss the process of receiving the Spirit and how to discern answers (and the commandment to honor and obey thy parents).

As you love, trust (but verify), enjoy, and listen to your teenager, the multitude of loving seeds will bear fruit at some juncture, either now or at a future harvest.

## Empty Nesters

Despite the challenges of age and an expanding family tree, I am often told with vigor that this is the best time of all. Grandparenting means wisdom, even if you wonder where your share went. For so many years you have loved your family and prayed for, worked for, and guided them to become fabulous future adults—now the rest is up to them. Though you can and should still be a source of peace and anchored testimony, your adult children will need the opportunity to grow, just like you did.

One challenge of this stage is to know when to help, advise, or step in, and how much. I am obviously not an empty nester, but my mother is. Over the years, she has given me two particularly great gifts: one, she does not comment on our parenting or marriage, and two, she does not do for us what we can do for ourselves.

These are two tough things for any grandparent—you see the need or the direction someone is headed, and you want to suggest something, step in, and make it smooth. But the greatest gift for your children then is to prayerfully consider your actions and carefully move forward a bit at a time. Whether it's loaning money, allowing them to live in your home, tending their children, or interceding in a difficult situation, loving wisely is a good thing. Grandparents are wise when they do what the Lord wants and feels is best for that particular situation.

**A suggestion.** One priceless thing you can do for any situation is to leave a spiritual legacy. You leave this legacy simply by what you watch, the activities you support, and the way you love and exemplify the gospel.

To further develop your legacy, share your personal talents. There's no need to look way *out there* for a cause, the Lord needs you *right here*! Use your particular gifts in your ward, stake, and branches. Continue doing family history, performing temple work, and serving missions. The Lord needs you to build His kingdom using the gifts and talents you still possess. Ask Heavenly Father how you can particularly serve with your physical or financial situation, even if it does take you to places unknown.

Elder Robert D. Hales shared the many wonderful things older couples have done: in India, helping a school for the blind receive braille typewriters; in Peru, organizing medicine and toys for over 500 orphans; and in Ghana, creating wells to bring water to 190,000 people.[11]

Be brave, follow through, and your example will create miracles.

## Wrapping Up

We've gone through many ideas for balancing motherhood. Let the ideas simmer while you sift through what matters most to you, right now, scooping up what consistently surfaces. You can have more balance in the daily tasks, trials, and triumphs of motherhood. And it doesn't have to require every last bit of energy or be a burden. Enjoy the spiritual filler that He provides for our parenting gaps. Do it His way and you will reap the rewards of eternity.

## Suggested Weekly Goals for Finding Balance in Motherhood

### *Create Vital Family Traditions*

- Choose three fun, creative ways to do scripture study and do one this week.
- Decide on a regular time for family prayer, ideally both in the morning and in the evening.
- At dinner or Family Home Evening, discuss ideas for family fun. Make a list and post it on the refrigerator. Then enjoy!

### *Raising Children as Future Adults*

- Set aside quiet time daily—perhaps fifteen to thirty minutes—and set appropriate rules to help your family respect it.
- Teach your children life skills by choosing one task to delegate to them (for example, mentor a sibling with homework).

### *Different Stages of Motherhood*

- Schedule a small block of time to develop a talent or pursue a hobby each week.
- Ask your teenager's advice on a family issue—listen, validate, and use something he or she has suggested.
- Create a spiritual legacy for your children in a way that is meaningful to you.

## Notes

Quote at chapter start found in M. Russell Ballard, "Daughters of God," *Ensign*, May 2008, 108–10.

1. Ibid.
2. First Presidency letter; *Church News*, Feb. 27, 1999, 3.
3. Cheryl C. Lant, "Righteous Traditions," *Ensign*, May 2008, 13–14.

4. Chieko N. Okazaki, *Lighten Up* (Salt Lake City: Deseret Book, 1993), 17.
5. Sharon G. Larsen, *All Rain, No Mud* (Salt Lake City: Deseret Book, 2005), 34.
6. Ballard, "Daughters of God," 108–10.
7. Ibid.
8. Larsen, *All Rain, No Mud*, 34.
9. Robert D. Hales, "With All the Feeling of a Tender Parent: A Message of Hope to Families," *Ensign*, May 2004, 90.
10. Harold B. Lee, "Love at Home," chap. 14 in *Teachings of Presidents of the Church: Harold B. Lee* (Salt Lake City: The Church of Jesus Christ of Latter-day Saints, 2000), 129.
11. Robert D. Hales, "Couple Missionaries: Blessings from Sacrifice and Service," *Ensign*, May 2005, 39–42.

six

# get organized!

"Thou shalt not idle away thy time, neither shalt thou bury thy talent that it may not be known"

D&C 60:13

Organization. Some of you are drooling (Type-A people), and some of you are bracing for pain.

Good news—there isn't any pain. In fact, you'll likely get done and say, "Is that it?" And while you're at it, "Wow, that's completely doable!" and possibly, "*No way*, I can't *wait* to try this."

Scripture tells us that organization is a spiritual foundation as well as a daily help. The earth was created in seven time periods. The Savior organized intelligences (Abraham 3:22). And all things were created spiritually first, then temporally (Moses 3:5). There is structure even in time and space. If we just go willy-nilly through life, we'll waste a good part of it on things that don't matter.

So how do we use our time and space wisely? The scriptures also say to "organize yourselves; prepare every needful thing" (D&C 88:119). But of all that needs organizing, what is needful? The answer is one that only you and the Lord know, so break it down to first things first.

Most women want to simplify the following: time, space, and family life. Each is addressed in this chapter with a few suggestions. You may be tempted to try all three areas at once, but please don't! Choose one area and rejoice in it. Then build on that foundation.

## Organize Your Time

Sister Julie B. Beck said that a good woman knows she doesn't have enough time or energy to do all the worthy things commanding her attention. But she notes that with personal revelation, each of us can understand priorities and learn how to effectively navigate our lives.[1]

We only have twenty-four hours and thankfully not a minute more—because we wouldn't organize it any better than we organize what we have now. But in those twenty-four hours, the Lord can make miracles happen, lengthening a minute or an hour in perplexing ways. We can garner more time, both spiritually and temporally, if we exercise faith and plan wisely. Translation: choose your priorities.

Sister Julie B. Beck states that when priorities are out of order, we lose power. Through personal prayer and study, she felt inspired to create three categories: essential, necessary, and nice-to-do.[2] Essentials are seeking revelation, scripture study, personal prayer, and service. Necessary items are homemaking, cooking, and supporting her husband. Nice-to-dos include recreation, hobbies, lunch with friends, and so forth.

Take heart. Sister Beck also said that while there's much to do, it amazes her how often she gets to her nice-to-do list, as long as priorities have been finished first.[3]

The art of time management is determining what is essential, necessary, and nice-to-do in *your* life. Then you can expend the right amount of energy on that particular task.

### Back to Basics—Go!

On a piece of paper, write the days of the week across the top. List the hours of the day down the left-hand side. Add your most typical tasks in a given week (for example, laundry, errands, cleaning, and so on). Next, consider which of these are Essentials, Necessities, or Nice-to-do. If you desire, circle and categorize them with colored markers.

Look at what you've written. Take a deep breath. Worry not. You can simplify using one of the following time-saving tips.

### Three Keys to Saving Time

You *have* extra time in your life, right now. These golden time chunks are just waiting to be discovered, so try one of these time-saving principles: Find the Why, Carve Out Time Chunks, and Be a B+.

**Key #1: Find the Why.** Why do you want to get organized? ("To find the kitchen counter"). Until you're clear on why you're saving time, nothing will motivate or sustain your organization goals. What would you do with *one* extra hour? Ten extra hours? What about twenty-six extra hours?

Years ago, I wanted to create a program that helped women and families get back to the center. I streamlined weekly tasks and found twenty-six free hours, using part of it to pursue my goal. The why gave me focus.

How we choose to spend our time is essential. In his book *Temple Worship*, Andrew Skinner recounted the following story from Archibald F. Bennett:

> Sister Susa Young Gates . . . once asked her father [Brigham Young] how it would ever be possible to accomplish the great amount of temple work that must be done, if all are given a full opportunity for exaltation. He told her there would be many inventions of labor-saving devices, so that our daily duties could be performed in a short time, leaving us more and more time for temple work. The inventions have come, and are still coming, but many simply divert the time gained to other channels, and not for the purpose intended by the Lord.[4]

This changed my life. I set a goal to attend the temple weekly and have continued to do so, regularly achieving it with many tender mercies and even with six children. It has profoundly blessed my family through increased peace, clarity, patience, and love. I'm not suggesting each person needs to attend the temple weekly for those benefits—circumstances and temple proximity make a difference—only perhaps to attend one more time than we currently do.

In the exercise below, brainstorm fun, purposeful, or motivating things you would love to do with your soon-to-be-free time. Complete a project or take a break—it's up to you!

For example:

### Fabulous Free Time

| 1 Hour | 5 Hours | 10 Hours |
|---|---|---|
| Read a book | Hike in nature | Create a craft corner at home |
| Do lunch with a friend | Attend the temple weekly | Do a FUN workout |
| Rest or take a nap | Scrapbook family pictures | Create a scripture sanctuary |

Now you try:

### Fabulous Free Time

| 1 Hour | 5 Hours | 10 Hours |
|---|---|---|
| | | |
| | | |
| | | |

**Key #2: Carve Time Chunks.** You *can* save time; you just have to want it. Bad. Badly enough that you say bye-bye to aimless web-surfing or endless social networking (save over five hours a week), repetitive grocery shopping (two hours), and continual tidying (five hours). Without radical lifestyle changes, you can save twelve hours a week. Try it!

Below, list suspected time wasters in a given week and honestly estimate how much you do them (one woman discovered two hours a day spent surfing online).

| Time Wasters | Total Time Spent |
|---|---|
| | |
| | |
| | |

Eliminate these time wasters by reducing or stopping them. If you're driving to several children's events, try organizing a carpool, driving two children in the same time slot, or allowing only one sport per year. If it's too much TV, record a show or limit yourself to one per night. If it's endless tidying, establish a family ten-minute pick-up after dinner or before bed. Add an incentive for the child done first and best. Then celebrate—one idea could save you three to four hours.

Wasted time is a gold mine of free hours. For example, at one point I wanted to resume writing but had six children, seventeen and under (the situations don't change, just the ages). Once again, I searched my schedule and discovered that my children's lessons—ballet and art—could provide needed writing time while I sat in the parental wings. Though the time was short, it was ideal—while the girls developed their talents, I developed mine.

Did those few hours make a difference? Combined with extra hours while my youngest attended preschool, I saved twenty hours a month for about three months. Using that time, I wrote the first major section of this book.

Now eliminate a time waster this week. Then select a positive time spender from your "Fabulous Free Time" chart.

1. This week I will eliminate ________ hours of wasted time by

   ______________________________________________.

2. I will use the new free time to ______________________

   ______________________________________________.

Maintain those new great habits and enjoy!

**Key #3: Be a B+.** Years ago I read this life-changing quote in *The Challenging Child* by Stanley Greenspan.

"Sometimes the best you can do is less than your 'best.' . . . For the first time in [parents'] lives, they face a situation where it is suddenly impossible to get an A or A+ on every subject at home and on the job. . . . [They] may have to consciously strive to do only a good-enough job . . . to deliberately stop short of [their] best in order to ensure that spouse and children get their fair share."[5]

It's amazing: being a B+ woman helps me accomplish more and feel happier. Use this mind-set to plan a reunion, organize a Church activity, or help at your child's school. No need to worry about the color of plastic silverware. Anytime you feel stress rise, cool it down with the refreshing knowledge that many things can appropriately be a B+ and still turn out great.

Another caveat: it is *not* wise to be a B+ in areas that require an A in order to properly function, such as tithing, honesty, fidelity in marriage, and so on. But for other definite B+ things—folding towels, weeding the backyard, organizing a spice cupboard—being a B+ is A-OK.

You've finished three keys to saving time: Find the Why, Carve Time Chunks, and Be a B+. Stop here! Choose one area for your Weekly Goal and move on to "Wrapping Up."

## Organize Your Space

Organizing your space is not what's daunting. It's *maintaining* the organization that feels like climbing Mount Everest. Repeatedly. After trial and tribulation, I created a one-formula-fits-all to help me get and stay organized. I've used it for years and it works for everything—from preparing a talk to cleaning out the garage to planning a trip.

### VEERS

VEERS is an acronym for three steps:

1. Visualize and Evaluate
2. Eliminate and Replace
3. Savor and Sustain

**Step #1: Visualize and Evaluate.** Envision how you want the space to look and function. Evaluate the activities that take place there. Group related activities into centers. Then effectively arrange those centers in the room.

**Step #2: Eliminate and Replace.** Clear and organize the actual space. Remove everything from the area and replace with only applicable items. Or simply remove what doesn't belong.

**Step #3: Savor and Sustain.** Keep the space functioning properly. Teach people using the space how the routine works. Follow up as needed to maintain it.

Simplicity is beauty—that's VEERS. Let's try it on an overflowing kitchen counter. (If you have children, you've got one.)

### *Visualize and Evaluate*

First, sit in a cozy chair and spend a few minutes *only* visualizing the counter space in its ideal form. Evaluate what functional "centers" you need. For example, a phone and files for immediate information (school, church lists, and so on), a family calendar for scheduling, and folders for bills. At this point, it can be frustrating to visualize (because you haven't actually seen the counter since 1996), but just imagine.

Next, sketch out the counter as if it were clear. Add circles in places where centers should go and name them. Play with this sketch until centers are simple yet functional.

### *Eliminate and Replace*

Now comes the fun part. Bring a deep empty tub over to the counter. With one swoop of your arm, slide everything from the counter into the tub.

You're finished with "Eliminate."

Next, replace *only* those items that belong and put them in the appropriate "center." Later sort and stow the remaining tub items in their rightful place. For example, the phone book goes under the phone stand with the message pad that Bobby made in third grade. Bills are sorted into folders for Paid, To Be Paid, and To Be Filed in the Bills Center. A family calendar is placed above or near the phone for easy access. Add a few family photos in fun frames and a beautiful plant.

You're finished!

***Savor and Sustain***

For this final step, show your family the great and spacious kitchen counter. Explain "The New Norm,"—meaning Mom's got a new rule. Any backpacks, half-eaten apples, soccer cleats, or stinky gym shorts on said counter will be returned at a steep price of Mama's choosing—laundry, car washing, or cold cash.

Savor and Sustain is vital to any new process. You must "show and tell" for your family—show it, tell them how it works, rinse and repeat, rinse and repeat. They will get this, especially after paying a few steep prices.

That's the VEERS formula—simple and effective. Now you try. Choose a space to reclaim and apply the VEERS formula.

I will organize the ___________________________________.

Use a blank piece of paper and write down the VEERS formula. Visualize and Evaluate how the space should look or function and what activities will take place there. Group into centers. Physically eliminate all items or only those that don't belong. Replace with only necessary items. Savor your excellent work and Sustain it by explaining the new rhythm to your family.

Try this VEERS activity for any trouble spot. Compile sketched pages in a labeled binder (for example, "Mom's Fabulous Organization Binder—Keep Out"). When you tackle a new area, the information will be handy.

With VEERS, you know how to quickly and effectively organize your space. Stop here! Skip right to the goal suggestions at the end of the chapter to create your Weekly Goal.

## Organize Your Family—Quick Meals, Kids' Zones, Family Centers

What are your most stressful tasks in running a home? For most women, they include cooking, cleaning, and organizing family schedules and information.

Regarding homemaking skills, Sister Beck said that even mundane tasks such as tidying, cleaning, and cooking are necessary to keep the Spirit in our homes. As we do them, we invest in our homes and families.[6]

It's wonderful that you can choose how to organize these activities. The following suggestions for quick meals, children's cleaning

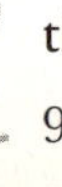

zones, and family information centers are simply that—suggestions. Enjoy doing what's best for your family.

## Quick Meals

In the early years of marriage, I loathed cooking. Then one day it hit me—cooking would be part of my life for many, many, many years. (Is there cooking in heaven? I seriously want to know.) But I discovered many hidden treasures in a consistent family dinner.

Elder Dallin H. Oaks shared that family mealtimes have proven effective against children's smoking, drinking, or using drugs, and adds that what most children desire for dinner is their parents' attention.[7] Family dinner is ideal for creating connection. It's when we can debrief and regroup (in the form of loud, chaotic, often obnoxious conversation).

While most of us agree with its importance, it's the doing that's stressful. How do we create a dinnertime—not just grab-and-go from the sideboard—in the middle of varying schedules and deadlines? Try two methods: involve the family and make it efficient. Do these two things and you'll love family dinner (okay, like it more).

**1. Involve your family.** Cooking is not a mom thing, it's a family thing. According to ability, all children should help. Little ones can set the table with place mats, silverware, and cups. Older children can be sous-chefs—cutting, boiling, and making. Follow the axiom of give a child a fish (and he'll say, "Phee-ew, what *is* that?") and you feed him for a day. Teach him how to cook and you can relax and say, "Good job."

List a few meals, simple and more advanced, to teach your older children (and they in turn teach the younger ones). Simple meals can be soup and sandwiches, spaghetti, tacos, slow cooker meals, and so on. It won't be pretty, but it will be purposeful. This is about practice and progress, so have fun with it. Put on music or use a special apron. We use a poufy white chef's hat. Involve your children, teach them a life skill, and eventually you'll feel good about dinnertime.

**2. Make it efficient.** When I quit whining about cooking (mostly) and let go of lofty culinary ideals, I discovered my meal method—fast, nutritious, and easy to clean up. Retooling fifteen favorite recipes, I had healthy ingredients and simple steps (download recipes at www.8basics.com).

Let's try retooling lasagna. Rather than having to simmer an Italian sauce (all day), buy ricotta cheese (a trip to the store), and brown ground beef (another ten minutes), simplify it. Try Paul Newman's "Sockarooni" sauce (includes pureed veggies), low-fat cottage cheese, low-fat mozzarella cheese, and a mixture of wheat and semolina lasagna noodles. It's healthy, delicious, and can be assembled by children in less than ten minutes.

## Kids' Zones

Mothers don't need more practice loading, folding, or tidying—but children do. If you have children—especially older than five—you've graduated to Chore Supervisor (translation: train, then help with the last ten percent). Children need to realize that they're part of a family, and a family is messy.

This is where "The Mom" comes in, and you need to be clear. Look around your home, apartment, or car, and identify trouble spots (no fair saying, "All of it"). Simply start with three drive-you-crazy clutter spots—perhaps the entry, kitchen, and main bathroom.

These now become Zones—areas in your home to be cleaned on a certain day and a certain number of times a week. Once assigned (and modeled a few times by you or an older child) the Zone is the child's responsibility. Typically, it is tidied every day and deep cleaned once a week. Match a zone with a child's age or abilities. For clarity, type or post pictures on a job card—a three- to five-step process instructing how to clean that zone—and post it nearby. Feel free to keep it simple—it's a job card, not a master's thesis.

Once the Zone is assigned and modeled, explain the Job Card. Let them do the job and, if needed, help them complete it (yes, this means you'll do it twice over). After this mentoring, children can generally clean alone with minimal supervision. If it takes all day, that's okay, just don't get roped into doing it (ask for their best try).

For example, one of our Zones is the family room, and this is the job card:

### *Family Room Job Card*

1. Pick up all trash
2. Quick tidy: replace cushions, fold blankets, stack books, put toys away

3. Put items that don't belong where they belong
4. Vacuum the floor
5. Dust the shelves, tables, and TV armoire

Job cards clarify expectations. In this case, the first three items are daily tasks; the last two are done once-a-week for deep cleaning.

Zones can be done different ways. Vacuuming can be its own Zone to avoid everyone needing the vacuum simultaneously. Or two children can share a Zone—a younger child with an older one. Ideally, you could rotate Zones every two weeks (less confusion and complaints). Choose a day for deep cleaning that works best for you and your family's schedule.

To introduce the Zones, make it a game (even for teens). During Family Home Evening, set the timer, and in pairs have children 1) choose a job card, 2) follow cleaning instructions, and 3) complete the chore first and best. The winner receives a three-scoop make-your-own-sundae or whatever works. During the week, keep motivation high with a random tasty treat or a thirty-minute fun time to the person who is finished first and best. It's amazing how the promise of a popsicle improves cleanliness.

Give it a whirl. Write down trouble spots—now officially renamed Zones—make job cards, mentor young children, and celebrate the success (or attempt thereof).

## Family Centers

Are your children's book orders, homework lists, and scout records in places unknown? Today, the "Where is it?" wonder is over. Your Family Center is the communication hub. Big or small, whiteboard or bulletin board, it matters not. Use what fits you and your family. Two essential parts to a Family Center are a family calendar and a family board.

**Family Calendar.** Our calendar is fixed to our fridge (the busiest place in the house), and I not only use it for scheduling family life, but on the blank squares I also record mom reminders like "Buy," "Do," and "Projects This Month." All family activities and needs are listed in one place.

During Family Home Evening, run through the weekday schedule, and as each child details activities, record them. Now the family knows everyone's events and can include them in personal prayers—a test, a ball game, or attending the temple. As children use a family calendar, they'll better use their own planners. They'll also learn that if an event isn't written down, it doesn't exist, despite wailing and gnashing of mouth guards.

**Family Boards.** A bulletin board in the kitchen or main area keeps vital family information close by. Our family uses a big bulletin board visually split into vertical thirds for 1) family mission statement and goals, 2) general family info—projects, reading calendars, book reports—and 3) children's church packets (big envelopes cut in half that hold Faith in God/Duty to God booklets, letters from church leaders, scout information, and so on).

Do what works best for you. Simply choose a handy spot and then visualize and evaluate the information you need handy. Clear the space if needed and replace it with a board. If not a board, try something else—clipboards, envelopes, binders, magazine holders, and small tubs work just as well. Whichever you choose, keep it in one place and organized in labeled sections.

## Wrapping Up

You've made it through fabulous organizing information, congratulations! Now comes the hard part—choosing your Weekly Goal. You've learned the 3 Keys to Saving Time, the VEERS formula for space organization, and how to organize your family with quick meals, chores, and centers. Choose the most urgent or what brings the greatest relief and make one Weekly Goal. Enjoy the time saved with a fun or functional activity!

## Suggested Weekly Goals to Get Organized!

### *Time*

- Make a time chart outlining essential, necessary, and nice-to-do activities.
- Choose one of the 3 Keys to Saving Time.
- Complete the Time Waster chart and discover free time already in your schedule.

### *Space*

- Use the VEERS formula on one clutter spot in your home.
- Buy and prepare a personal binder to organize all information, sketches, and records.

### *Family*

- Create a more efficient and healthy version of six favorite family meals.
- Assign a children's cooking night once a week.
- Visit www.8basics.com and try a Basic Meal that appeals to you (for example, 3-minute fajitas).
- Sketch an ideal family board. What information do you need handy? What needs to be tracked weekly and monthly?
- Identify three clutter spots and make them into Zones. Type a simple job card for each zone and post it nearby.

## Notes

1. Julie B. Beck, "And upon the Handmaids in Those Days Will I Pour Out My Spirit," *Ensign*, May 2010, 10–12.
2. Julie B. Beck, BYU Women's Conference, April 29, 2010.
3. Ibid.

4. Andrew C. Skinner, *Temple Worship: 20 Truths That Will Bless Your Life* (Salt Lake City: Deseret Book, 2007), 145.
5. Stanley Greenspan, *The Challenging Child* (New York: Addison-Wesley, 1995), 294–95.
6. Julie B. Beck, BYU Women's Conference, April 29, 2010.
7. Dallin H. Oaks, "Good, Better, Best," *Ensign*, Nov. 2007, 104–8.

seven

# create healthy connections

"The family isn't just the basic unit of society; it is the basic unit of eternity."

M. Russell Ballard

Think back to a happy memory. What were you doing? What were you feeling? No matter the event or experience, it likely included another person. Now reflect on a deeply painful memory and ask the same questions—once again, it probably involved another person.

Relationships are everything. The earth was created for families. Friendship can get us through the day. And after our children are grown, eternal marriage will bind us all together in the end.

But relationships can be Dickensian—the best of times and the worst of times. We need each other, but it's the getting along that's stressful. So how do we negotiate the difficulties to more fully enjoy healthy relationships? The next three sections offer ideas to improve relations with your spouse, children, and friends (with the emphasis on marriage). As always, please choose *one* area to focus on! Obviously, eighteen pages about connection is not a definitive work on relationships. The principles in this chapter are springboards to begin feeling and behaving in more healthy ways.

## Marriage

One of my favorite cartoons about marriage is from the book *Why We'll Never Understand Each Other* by cartoonist Wiley Miller.

What he heard: "Honey, why don't you put your head in a vise and I'll turn the handle until your skull explodes."

What she said: "Honey, why don't we turn off the TV and just talk?"[1]

In marriage we have similarities and differences in perceptions, backgrounds, values, and opinions. We also have different growth timelines—the rate and depth at which we progress. Living with varying mortal schedules requires love, and lots of it. But that's a good thing because we're here to learn to love like God. We don't white-knuckle it through marriage—enduring to the end—then sigh with relief that it's over. Marriage is a developing process, and you and I are becoming better people through it. If we're not, we're missing the mark.

Two things before we begin. First, I know that every marital relationship is unique: some have regular ups and downs, some are struggling, and some are hanging on by their marital fingernails. The following suggestions will help any marriage: Cling to Your Covenants, Communicate with Clarity, and Create Connection. But for those with serious issues such as abuse, adultery, and addiction, I strongly encourage you to seek help from appropriate Church leaders, since these are difficult to deal with on your own.

Second, the marriage section can be condensed into two words: change first. This doesn't suggest that you are the problem or that your spouse isn't in need of change. It simply means to stop focusing negatively on your spouse and begin focusing on what *you* can do to create change in the marriage.

## Cling to Your Covenants

Bruce C. Hafen said that when we keep our sacred covenants, we discover hidden strength.[2]

My mother shared with me a powerful revised version of the Serenity Prayer:

"God grant me the serenity to accept the things I cannot change; courage to change the things I can; and the wisdom to know [that it is me]." Anonymous

But then I came across an even more helpful version that Mary Ellen Edmunds once saw on a poster:

"Grant me the serenity to know what I can change. Let me change what I can. Let me accept that which I cannot change. Let me ignore that which I cannot change or accept. Let me run away from that which I cannot change, accept, or ignore. Let me lock myself in the bathroom, hold my hands over my ears, and hum about that which I cannot change, accept, ignore, or run away from. Let me bite those who can change, accept, ignore, run. Let me be!"[3]

Whatever frustration or difficult situation comes your way, stay focused on clinging to your covenants—they are made with God, your husband, and yourself. No matter the examples around you, *your* path is to be faithful to His will. The adversary works tirelessly to convince you that things are hopeless, that they will never change. But that is a lie. President Monson once shared a story about a prison warden who worked with inmates who were considered to be hopeless. A skeptical reporter commented to the warden that leopards didn't change their spots. The warden replied that he didn't work with leopards, he worked with men; and men changed every day.[4]

We can add "women" in that sentence as well. In the triangular relationship of marriage—the Lord, your spouse, and you—there are two people who need to change. Pray for the Lord to create that change. Plead for love and strength and perspective—the eternal kind. He will help you see "things as they really are" (Jacob 4:13), including yourself.

**A Love List.** At times we magnify our spouse's negative traits until they fill our viewfinder. But these are good men. They work to the bone for their families, spend hours on Church work and in meetings, and walk in the door after a difficult day only to be told to fix the washer and hold family scripture study. Repeatedly they are told by many people—bosses, clients, employees—that they're not good enough and that they're failing at something. Men are looking for a soft place to fall. We can choose to listen to the Lord and, like Emma, "be for a comfort unto my servant . . . thy husband, in his afflictions, with consoling words, in the spirit of meekness" (D&C 25:5).

Nurturing our spouse nurtures ourselves. Providing a warm dinner and a tidy home—these aren't extravagant gifts, but they're meaningful and respectful. At times I hear women complain about having to cook, clean, and keep things organized (that wouldn't be me).

Complain we can—though an occasional vent is much more healthy—but do we must. And I don't mean that to be chorelike.

My husband didn't delight in edging hardwood floors, but he did it because it provided for our family. Homemaking is our office, and as we joyfully approach it, our marriage will be blessed. President James E. Faust said that when obedience is our focus, it ceases to be an irritation.[5]

To paraphrase: when nurturing our spouse becomes our goal, it will cease to become an irritation. This doesn't exclude appropriately caring for our own souls. But it does put life in the proper sequential order.

## Back to Basics—Go!

To help maintain that order, create a Love List—a page-long list of traits and characteristics you love about your spouse. Think back to how you met, kind things he has said or done, and experiences you've shared together. Post the Love List where you can read it daily. In a needful moment, a Love List brings me back to emotional center: by number ten, I feel warm fuzzies; by number twenty-two, I'm in tears. By number thirty-seven, I'm putting candles on the table and eagerly awaiting his return.

Marriage is not about what's fair, equal shares, or immediate rewards. It's about focusing on the right things—kindness, respect, and loving as the Lord loves.

In *To Draw Closer to God*, President Henry B. Eyring told a story about his father fulfilling a welfare assignment by weeding at the Church farm. Suffering from advanced hip cancer and barely able to walk, he spent the hot day pulling weeds by lying on his belly and pushing himself forward with his elbows. That afternoon, someone stopped by and told Brother Eyring that he had weeded the wrong spot—the weeds had been sprayed with chemicals and would have died in a few days. Brother Eyring burst out laughing at his mistake and later told his son, President Eyring.

But his son responded, "'Dad, how could you make a joke out of that? How could you take it so pleasantly?' He said something to me that I will never forget, and I hope you won't. He said, 'Hal, I wasn't there for the weeds.'"[6]

This is marriage. We are not here for the immediate perfection of events or people. We're here to serve and love and do what is right, trusting in the Lord with all our hearts, and leaning not unto our own understanding (Proverbs 3:5). The Lord will heal your heart and make your burdens light. Just like He did for the Lamanites being persecuted by Amulon (Mosiah 24:13–15).

Despite their unfair treatment and circumstances, the Lamanites remained faithful to the Lord, *working* and *praying* for deliverance. But it wasn't immediate; they had some things to learn from this experience. First He eased the burdens; *then* He delivered them. Because the Lamanites remained true to their covenants, the Lord was able to bless them and ultimately deliver them.

Elder Bruce C. Hafen has said:

> When troubles come, the parties to a contractual marriage seek happiness by walking away. They marry to obtain benefits and will stay only as long as they're receiving what they bargained for. But when troubles come to a covenant marriage, the husband and wife work them through. They marry to give and to grow, bound by covenants to each other, to the community, and to God. Contract companions each give 50 percent; covenant companions each give 100 percent. Marriage is by nature a covenant, not just a private contract one may cancel at will.[7]

A friend of mine learned a pivotal lesson about marriage while single and on a mission. She served in a foreign country where the people were generally short, and my friend happened to be particularly tall. With her long legs, she outpaced her smaller companion, which made her wait. Often. And this bothered my friend. A lot. One day they both ran to catch a needed bus. My friend outstripped her and was almost to the bus when she had a strong impression. "You can't get on that bus without your companion." She understood the layered message and waited for her companion to reach the same spot.

Marriage is not a race. It's a journey to learn to love as God loves and to fulfill sacred covenants through the guidance of the Holy Spirit. Then we reap and enjoy eternal blessings with those we love.

## Communicate with Clarity: Use a Value Scale and a 1-2-3 Check

Communication makes women salivate and grown men shudder. But the problem lies on both sides. When a woman finally gets the whites of his eyes, she goes long and hard, listing everything from being a better listener to building a new addition. On the flip side, a man struggles to accept that a random comment or a back-of-the-head view is not considered conversation.

How do we meet in the middle? Try a value scale and a three-step check.

### *The Value Scale*

Let's say the garbage is an issue—frustrating to the wife, not so much to the husband. An average conversation may go like this:

"Honey, the garbage is spilling out all over the yard."

"Uh hm." (He continues reading.)

"And it's messing up the yard and the neighborhood dogs are getting into it." (Evidence of a just claim.)

"Uh hm."

"And really, no one in the family knows who's supposed to take it out, or when, or how it's supposed to be done." (Showing the crux of the problem, in case he missed it.)

Silence.

"The neighbors have mentioned it. Several times." (Going for peer pressure.)

"Is that right?" (Still reading.)

"You know," (the trump card), "our neighbor always has his garbage neatly organized on the curb; maybe you could ask how he does it."

Complete, deafening silence.

"Fine then." (Utter defeat.) "I'll just do it myself." (Banging of assorted pots, pans, and cupboard doors in the kitchen.)

Husband looks up from reading, hears the racket, and moves to the peace and privacy of his den.

Ah, marital communication.

The core of the problem is the value scale. For her the garbage is a 10—it's keeping her up at night. For him, it's maybe a 3—garbage is just a fact of life, so what if it spills? Whether it's mowing the lawn or overspending, the actual *thing* doesn't matter—it's how both people value it.

Elder L. Tom Perry said,

> Remember, brethren, that in your role as leader in the family, your wife is your companion. As President Gordon B. Hinckley has

> taught: "In this Church the man neither walks ahead of his wife nor behind his wife but at her side. They are coequals." . . . Therefore, there is not a president or a vice president in a family. The couple works together eternally for the good of the family. . . . They are on equal footing. They plan and organize the affairs of the family jointly and unanimously as they move forward.[8]

Choose an issue or event that is stressful and have each person rate it on a scale of 1 to 10. For her, the cactus in the yard is a 10; for him, it's a 2.

If you're truly not, in any form, interested in what is important to your spouse, try raising the value on your side by one level, say from a 2 to a 3. Regardless of your personal feelings, show more interest in and respect for your spouse's needs and desires. If it's not breaking a covenant or compromising morals, then it's just about validating what matters to your spouse.

Early in our marriage, my husband often reminded me to change the oil in the car. But for several years, I forgot. Although I had stellar memory recall in other areas, this particular request didn't register. Why was oil so important, I wondered, and why did it need to be changed so often? How did the time required to change it compare to essential things, like cookies for the Relief Society meeting or a parent-teacher conference?

But one day, I got it. I don't recall why, but it hit me—oil is key to the car running smoothly (that sound you hear is men all over the world cheering). So before you roll your eyes at his lack of understanding (for example, missing Bobby's science fair or dressing Sally in mismatched clothes), consider my husband's eye-rolling restraint. Rather than make me feel inept, he simply expressed appreciation for getting the oil changed. Raising my value scale to increase my respect for his needs or desires led to a functioning car.

But what if you reach an impasse—you're at a 10 and he's at a 2, and he will never want that cactus in the yard? Consider if it's really a 10 *compared* to your marriage. Is that cactus worth causing a fuss? Remember the adage, "Is this the hill you want to die on?" Serious issues like gambling, pornography, and theft are definitely a 10 and can't suddenly be a 2. But things like where you spend Christmas or what you plant in the yard are definitely negotiable.

### *The 1-2-3 Check*

You've discussed, compromised, value-scaled, and now you both definitely agree: having corn-on-the-cob at the July 4th party is a 10. Maybe an 11.

So far so good.

But the day of the party arrives, and so does your husband, but without the corn. What do you do? This very thing happened to my husband and I. It was so life-changing that I wrote a newspaper column about it. Here is an excerpt:

> We went back out together to get the corn (not that I was supervising) and as we got closer to the nearest city, I saw the first stand—completely empty. (Gasp) "There's not going to be corn?" I said. "All right. It's okay,"—like it was self-therapy or something. I felt my heart thump, my blood pressure rise, and pretty much my whole world collapse because of the ABSENCE OF CORN. My husband said, "No worries. WE WILL FIND THE CORN,"—and proceeded forth like John Smith in exploration. That's when it hit me—WHY AM I BEING SO RIDICULOUS ABOUT CORN ON THE COB? Why was I having such a meltdown about this and making my husband feel like a failure and giving myself hives over a starchy vegetable?

As women, before we do anything, we can relax. Is it life-threatening? Is it immoral? Is it a starchy vegetable? We can bring it back to reality. I'm not saying that as women we can be oversensitive (a hormonal swing every thirty minutes), or that men are casual about requests (research shows that men don't value to-do lists). I am saying it's *highly possible* that we are overreacting. Once there is calm—and a real need to further resolve an issue—then try the 1-2-3 Check.

**Step 1: Validate.** Gary and Joy Lundberg, authors of *I Don't Have to Make Everything All Better*, state that validation is to listen, listen, listen, and understand.[9] In a difficult situation, the last thing your spouse needs is an I-told-you-so lecture. Validate with calm phrases like, "I'm so sorry that happened," or, "That must have been so frustrating," or even, "I can understand how you might have felt that way." And then go tenderize some meat.

Whether he's late (again) or bounced a check (again), simply validate. Do not make accusations, suggestions, or sarcastic comments. Ask the Lord to help you remove negative feelings. Anger is exactly what the adversary wants because it clouds our judgment and makes marriage become a "you versus him" situation. It's not. We don't know what private hurts your spouse conceals. Just because you verbalize everything doesn't mean he does or even wants to. In a maddening moment, only focus on being a loving, stellar wife. Later, you will address the actual issue once the irrational urge to smash dishes has passed.

Keep some natural-sounding validation phrases handy: "I'm sorry," "I can see how you would think that," or "That's so frustrating." Give it a try and save the dishes.

**2. Make reasonable requests.** Something that's negatively affecting a couple or family needs to be discussed, decided, or done. Perhaps it's fixing a washer, helping a child with homework assignments, or being on time. So make a reasonable request.

First, be prayerful that the request is reasonable. Then together as a couple, complete a Value Scale. But what if you've followed this process, and nothing is being done?

A reasonable request could sound like this: "This week, I would really like to clean up the yard. I'm thinking it will take about two hours. Do you want to split that between weeknights or do it all on a Saturday?" Together, choose a day and time that works best. If the agreed day comes and your spouse doesn't remember, isn't interested, or flat-out won't do it, you have several options. You can point to an *Ensign* article about the difficulties of single life. You can stand with your hands on your hips, with the expression of a charging elk. You can sulk and slam kitchen cabinets.

Or you can say, "We planned to do the yard tonight with the kids. I know none of us really want to do it, but we agreed it needs to be done. Do you have any other solutions?" Discuss the possibilities. For example, maybe he says to do it another day. Perhaps you offer to call a landscape company. With kindness, assess the situation. If he's coming down with the flu, reschedule it. If this is the third time it's been rescheduled, set an agreeable deadline—if it's not done by Saturday, you'll hire the professionals.

That's a reasonable request. You're not pushing a personal agenda or asking for the moon. Something needs to be done in a reasonable time frame, and both of you are working toward the solution. If within a reasonable time a request is not fulfilled, then try something else. Try it his way. Try it your way. Try it a new way. Someone once said that dishes don't care what gender you are, they just need to be done.

However you solve it, show respect, even if you're not receiving it. Keep your dignity. I think of Nephi, watching his parents struggle through their family situation. At the lowest of lows, Lehi shows us—mercifully—that he is human, and he murmurs. (With Laman and Lemuel for sons, it's astonishing that this is the *first* we hear of murmuring). Nephi doesn't get angry, give him the cold shoulder, or say, "What kind of a priesthood holder are you?" He quietly finds a solution, makes a bow, and then goes to his father and asks where to find the food. In that gentle, decisive, but loving solution, his father is humbled and repents. If your spouse doesn't respond that same way, that's not the point. You have been valiant, you have done the right thing, and you and your family will be blessed.

**3. Risk Conflict.** This is not *incite* conflict—a big difference. Dr. John Gottman, author of *The Seven Principles for Making Marriage Work*, says that arguing in marriage is not necessarily destructive—it's the *way* that we argue that can be harmful.[10] Another big difference.

Back to the yard issue. Saturday comes and the yard remains untouched. Now you need to choose. Will you become angry and then retreat and feel helpless, or will you risk conflict and move forward on what was agreed upon? With love and the Spirit, you can risk conflict. Discuss the problem, give opportunity for a solution, and then move forward. If it comes down to calling the landscape company, it will likely create tension. But if you have both agreed, and it is not respected, will this tension ultimately lead to a positive result? Prayer and kindness will help you know.

For a few years, my husband and I differed on detailing the family car. Exhausted with four little ones, I wanted someone else to do it. Counting the extra cost, he felt the family could do it. After a few years of the family method, we realized it wasn't working. The rare times we attempted to clean the car, it consisted of my husband and I simultaneously cleaning and corralling young children armed with soap and a hose.

After making reasonable requests and attempting new solutions, nothing was adhered to or changed. Because this was a 10 on my value scale, I risked conflict and took the van to a detail shop. Afterward, it sparkled. I drove it to my husband's job site and said, "Look at this beautiful van. No Cheerios, no grease spots, no juice stains." He leaned in and said, "Wow, it looks great. Maybe I should get my truck done too."

As men and women, we're born to do things differently. It's purposeful. It can be annoying, but it's part of the Lord's plan, and He is wise. The sooner we work with this wise plan rather than complain against it, the sooner we will combine our strengths to create a positive, enjoyable result.

## Create Connection

When was the last time you and your spouse had *fun*? What were you doing? What would you like to do? As a couple, no matter your age, have fun together. Travel, garden, hike, cook—the list is endless. That's what friends do, and the most interesting long-term friends do interesting things together. Through shared pastimes we create opportunities to talk, laugh, and connect.

I invite you to go on a weekly date, just as we've been counseled numerous times by Church leaders and research alike. Even if you can't stand the sight of each other that particular day, go anyway.

If you don't like the same things, that's okay. We're married, not chained at the hip. We can compromise and delight in one another's fun. On a cruise my husband and I met another couple. The husband loved to scuba dive, and the wife loved to read. At one point in their marriage, she had certified for scuba. And hated it. So they made a deal: he would dive and she would read on the boat, waiting topside to hear the news afterward.

Remind yourselves why you got married. Hold hands, tell jokes, kiss like you used to. Create that emotional connection, and you'll find life's bumps don't bother you so much.

Every bit of nourishment poured upon your marriage will help it bear emotional fruit. "But if ye will nourish the word, yea, nourish the tree as it beginneth to grow, by your faith with great diligence, and with patience, looking forward to the fruit thereof, it shall take root; and behold it shall be a tree springing up unto everlasting life. . . . ye shall reap the rewards of your faith, and your diligence, and patience, and long-suffering, waiting for the tree to bring forth fruit unto you" (Alma 32:41, 43).

That wraps up the section on marriage—the largest one in the chapter, and for good reason. Choose *one* goal from Cling to Your Covenants, Communicate with Clarity, or Create Connection. Enjoy!

## Children

As a child, one of my sons was happy and easy-going. As he grew older, at one point I noticed he became slightly withdrawn and not as talkative (*before* his teen years). It wasn't severe, but after a period of time, I could see it wasn't changing. As a middle child of six children, I could see that he felt lost.

Seeking for help, I prayed, researched, and found helpful principles. One of them was Dr. Gary Chapman's *The Five Love Languages of Children*. Dr. Chapman states that these five languages are: quality time, words of affirmation, gifts, acts of service, or physical touch.[11] After assessing that my son's top languages were words of affirmation and touch, I chose to first focus on more specific praise. Then I created opportunities for him to talk to me, one-on-one. And when he was near, I touched him in a positive way—ruffled his hair, gave him a side hug, or scratched his back while he talked to me. The difference was immediate. Within days he became more responsive, within a week he was back to himself.

Knowing your child's love language can be life-changing. This is not about how *you* want to show love, it's about how *they* need to receive it. Most children need quality time, which is often the most difficult to give. But it doesn't have to be a production. We can look for typical opportunities to connect. Whether it's driving someone to a sporting event or creating a poster for a school report, we can use these moments to talk, laugh, and bond. When our son forgot his bike at the baseball field, my husband invited him to come along to pick it up. Though it was brief, their enjoyable experience added another connection coin to the emotional bank account.

Special nights are another great way to make children feel loved. Try a date night with your sons, and a girls' night out with your daughters. I've gone to the dollar movie and heard all about Lego construction with my boys; I've bought princess cookbooks and made spa scrubs with my girls. We also enjoy Gender Night—my husband takes the boys (all things sweaty), and I take the girls (all things delicious). Although we can mix up activities any way we like (sweaty and delicious), it's quality and fun time.

Find small and daily ways to fill your children's buckets. Post excellent school papers on the Family Board. Announce best efforts in an art contest, despite the outcome. Ask each other to pray for an upcoming event. Be creative. One mother put notes under her children's pillows. I tried this, but due to my boys' bizarre sleeping positions, the notes were never found. So I resorted to miniature red mailboxes for appreciation notes, holiday treats, and creative expressions of love.

Showing interest in their hobbies—regardless of your knowledge about them—pays superb emotional dividends. As they wax long about the latest tech toy, aviation jargon, or Tesla coils, your attempts at understanding and enthusiasm help them feel "I am loved, I matter, and I am good."

## Positive Responses

After returning home from a date one night, my husband and I discovered that our son, in our absence, had decided to wash the tiny ball bearing–like BBs for his BB gun. In the kitchen sink. And as we enquired about this choice, our son told us it was because the bee-bees were dirty, and that it had been a difficult process because he "couldn't see into the sink with those black flaps from the disposal." Solving this annoyance, he had cut them out. All of them.

In a stellar parenting moment, we explained—with great calm and detail—how removing the flaps caused the disposal to be indisposed. Then we asked how he would like to earn the money to replace the disposal. With a smile, we added that he now had a great opportunity to learn a new life skill—installing a new disposal with the help of his father.

When your children choose unwisely (note: *when*), be prepared. Choose an expression that mimics a catatonic rhino. Simply stare, nod, and say, "Is that right?" Unleash your fury at a later time—on an unsuspecting veal cutlet—but for the moment, remember that no matter the actual age, your child is still that—a child.

Elder Per G. Malm shared a story about his grandmother. She had sent one of her young children to buy some eggs. In what was likely a happy walk home, most of the eggs had been broken. Upon the child's arrival, a friend of his grandmother suggested the child be scolded for bad behavior. Instead, the grandmother said that doing so wouldn't make the eggs whole again. She then suggested they use what they had to make pancakes together.[12]

Responding with calmness and kindness allows our children to grow, make normal mistakes, and trust that we love and respect them. This is not about minimizing poor choices—appropriate consequences are wise teachers. This is about handling with care a fragile self-esteem.

### Back to Basics—Go!

Sister Gayle M. Clegg recounts that when her daughter was young, she asked her mother to play tetherball with her. After several minutes of just watching her repeatedly hit the ball on the rope, Sister Clegg asked what her part was in playing. The daughter said her mom's part was simply to say, "Good job."[13]

Apply this concept to your own children and try a positive-only day. For 24 hours, say only positive things to your child. I tried this. I'm a positive person, and my first time I made it to an hour. We may think that we're positive or, at the very least, not negative or simply getting things done. But functional point-and-shoot parenting can leave collateral damage.

Obviously, I'm not suggesting to be Snow White and sing the chore list. But it doesn't hurt to say, "Thanks so much for cleaning your room. Would you please finish up the bathroom?" or "Your towels are looking so good. Let me see how well you do your toy buckets." It takes practice. But if you're more positive today than you were yesterday, and the next day more positive than before, within a year you'll be smiling, and they'll have rediscovered their happy mother.

## Friendships

A few years ago, as a life coach, I did a regular short segment on a local morning show. One morning I had decided to talk on friends, which worried me as it seemed a seventh-grade topic for a high-powered morning show. In addition, I was not technically skilled. So my "visual aid" to graphically show the progression of closer friendships was a piece of white poster board with red concentric circles drawn by using various-sized pot lids.

Being my bold self, I followed instinct and went on the show.

To my knowledge, it received the most viewer response of any of my segments. Certainly not for the visual aid. Despite the tacky graph, women felt relieved to know that others felt alone, desired to know how to make new friendships, and felt motivated to strengthen their current ones.

No woman is an island, yet often we live busy, self-contained lives, leading us to feel that we don't have time for, nor immediately need, female friendship. But Sister Marjorie Pay Hinckley said it best:

"Oh, how we need each other. Those of us who are old need you who are young. And, hopefully, you who are young need some of us who are old. It is a sociological fact that women need women. We need deep and satisfying and loyal friendships with each other. These friendships are a necessary source of sustenance. . . . We need to lock arms and help build the kingdom so that it will roll forth and fill the whole earth."[14]

A whole chapter—an entire book—could be written on friendship. For brevity, I'll focus on understanding and strengthening the types of friendships in our lives.

## Nourishing Friendships

As women, we need varying levels of friendship. It's unhealthy to expect that each acquaintance will become a lifelong pal. For clarity, I've sorted friendships into three main categories: Casual, Connected, and Core. Think of them as three concentric circles (red, drawn with pot lids) becoming smaller as the intimacy progresses.

**Casual.** People we meet are most often at the fringes. We see them at community, social, or sporting events. Our connection ranges from a wave hello to regular life updates—what I call "touchpoints." The conversation may be at most five to ten minutes, but you connect and move on, like bouncing neurons and protons, meeting again at the next event.

**Connected.** These friendships have gained enough touchpoints over time or experience to create a deeper connection. These are women you could call when you need a lift or to share an important life event. You could go to lunch, share an emotional experience, and then not see them for months but feel fine about it.

**Core.** These friendships are lifelong and beyond. Even after years of being apart, you easily reconnect. You've shared bonding experiences like no other and rarely run out of things to say. When you do, the silence is comfortable. There is a rhythmic ebb and flow to your connection. These are the friends to treasure, yet they are the first to be slighted because you know they will always be there—they're the ones you call with news of cancer. It's only through growing older that we begin to comprehend the inestimable value of these friendships.

Although friends may currently be in one category, it's natural for relationships to experience cycles of closeness and distance, moving between circles throughout your life. But whatever their place, their presence is essential.

Now that you are aware of a few friendship types, let's focus on ways to strengthen them.

## Back to Basics—Go!

Consider your friends and their place in your life. Complete the following exercise.

1. List a few of your

Casual friends: ______________________________

Connected friends: ______________________________

Core friends: ______________________________

2. Choose one friend in each category you would like to be closer to.

Casual: ______________________________

Connected: ______________________________

Core: ______________________________

3. What is one thing you can do this week to nurture that friendship?

Casual: ______________________________

Connected: ______________________________

Core: ______________________________

Completing this exercise years ago was truly life-changing for me. I realized there were several friends I had neglected—counting on their kindness to understand my busy life. During this time, I happened to be visited by a Core friend, someone I'd known since I was 21. As we chatted, I mentioned two of our mutual friends—same story: wonderful women, busy lives. I suggested we call our friends (one was out of state). We did, and we set a date for a reunion within a few weeks—the first of an annual connection that remains to this day. Each year we "BYU Babes" go away for a weekender, and in pajamas or in heels, shopping or chatting, at the temple or at a hotel, we spend the weekend exchanging thoughts and ideas on life, family, and joy.

Pick up the phone, send a card, type an email. Think of those dear friendships and do something to nurture them today.

## Wrapping Up

Whether it's with marriage, children, or friends, you have some simple suggestions for increasing that vital connection. Choose one section and one way to make that happen this week. Dip into the spiritual and emotional reservoirs the Lord has placed around you. You'll be grateful you did.

C.S. Lewis once said, "It is a serious thing to live in a society of possible gods and goddesses, to remember that the dullest and most uninteresting person you can talk to, may one day be a creature which if you saw now, you would be strongly tempted to worship. There are no ordinary people; you have never talked to a mere mortal, next to the blessed sacrament itself, your neighbor is the holiest object presented to your senses."[15]

## Suggested Weekly Goals for Creating Healthy Connections

### *Marriage*

- Create a Love List about your spouse and post it on the wall.
- *Briefly* share the Value Scale with your spouse and try it on a non–hot-button issue first.
- Use one of the steps of the 1-2-3 Check (for example, Validate).
- Choose a fun activity together that you can both enjoy (for example, a cooking class or a four-wheeler trip).

### *Children*

- Determine your child's love language and choose one way to "speak" it.
- Have a positive-only day—speak only positive things to your child.

### *Friendship*

- Complete the friendship exercise to determine Casual, Connected, and Core friends.
- Choose one friend to reconnect with this week and one way to do it.

## Notes

Quote at chapter start found in Andrew C. Skinner, *Temple Worship: 20 Truths That Will Bless Your Life* (Salt Lake City: Deseret Book, 2007).

1. Wiley Miller, *Why We'll Never Understand Each Other* (Kansas City, MO: Andrews McMeel, 2003).
2. Bruce C. Hafen, "Covenant Marriage," *Ensign*, Nov. 1996, 26.
3. Mary Ellen Edmunds, *You Can Never Get Enough of What You Don't Need: The Quest for Contentment* (Salt Lake City: Deseret Book, 2005), 7.
4. Thomas S. Monson, "To the Rescue," *Ensign*, May 2001, 48.

5. James E. Faust, "Obedience: The Path to Freedom," *Ensign*, May 1999, 47.
6. Henry B. Eyring, *To Draw Closer to God* (Salt Lake City: Deseret Book, 1997), 102.
7. Bruce C. Hafen, "Covenant Marriage," *Ensign*, Nov. 1996, 26.
8. L. Tom Perry, "Fatherhood, an Eternal Calling," *Ensign*, May 2004, 69–72.
9. Gary and Joy Lundberg, *I Don't Have to Make Everything All Better.*
10. John Gottman, *The Seven Principles for Making Marriage Work* (New York: three Rivers Press, 1999), 15.
11. Gary Chapman, *The Five Love Languages of Children* (Chicago: Northfield Publishing, 2005), 28.
12. Per G. Malm, "Rest unto Your Souls," *Ensign*, Nov. 2010, 102.
13. Gayle M. Clegg, "The Finished Story," *Ensign*, May 2004, 15.
14. Marjorie Pay Hinckley, *Small and Simple Things* (Salt Lake City: Deseret Book, 1999), 254.
15. C.S. Lewis, "The Weight of Glory" sermon, 9.

*eight*

# establish financial peace and prosperity

"Money management should take precedence over money productivity."

Elder Marvin J. Ashton

Finances are a hot-button issue, no doubt about it. Elder Ashton cited an American Bar Association report that 89 percent of all divorces trace back to money.[1] Concerns touch every phase of money: being over budget or not having a budget, insurance, or a future plan. Other concerns include living paycheck to paycheck, not teaching children money concepts or value, or being unaware of money management principles.

As we approach this chapter, consider your main concerns about money and your beliefs, behaviors, and attitudes about it. These money roots can go deep and reach far back to childhood. Open your heart as to how and what you feel about money and why—it can change your life. Allow yourself to feel honest emotions as you read the sections on Self, Marriage, and Children. The Lord will help you be more aware and motivated to tweak or overhaul financial practices and help your family do the same.

Remember to choose *one* section that best applies to your particular needs right now.

## Build the Kingdom of God

Before we go into each section, we need to know the purpose of money. In the Book of Mormon it says:

"But before ye seek for riches, seek ye for the kingdom of God. And after ye have obtained a hope in Christ ye shall obtain riches, if ye seek them; and ye will seek them for the intent to do good—to clothe the naked, and to feed the hungry, and to liberate the captive and administer relief to the sick and the afflicted" (Jacob 2:18, 19).

We are stewards, not owners. At some point we will account for how we spend, save, and manage the money in our care. When we focus on getting rich, we lose perspective and the ability to be trusted. Money is not our object—salvation is, and to help others to receive that same blessing. As money becomes an idol—or a constant fixation—we begin to feel that all problems are solved by getting more. It siphons energy from the good we could do.

Elder Joseph B. Wirthlin said that focusing on material possessions not only possibly makes us build a bigger home than needed (with additional decorating "needs"), but also that these choices—even for the wealthy—may misdirect resources that would be more effectively used to help others and build the kingdom.[2]

Does that mean we can't enjoy the benefits of financial prosperity? Not at all. But it's in the intent and balance that we find a solution. "For where your treasure is, there will your heart be also" (Luke 12:34). When our hearts are set on the Lord, we are wise in knowing when and how to give, spend, and save.

## Finances: Self

A wise steward pays the Lord first. The following are three basic financial practices any individual can follow. I can't promise many things, but as you consistently do them, I promise you can experience peace.

### An Honest Tithe

Tithing has been around since the Old Testament days of Abraham, who gave his tithes to Melchizedek. The principle is to pay one-tenth of our increase, or gross earnings. Most of us know this tithing principle. The personal question of what constitutes "increase" is largely left for us to prayerfully decide. But do we fully comprehend the Lord's promises in return for obedience? In the Bible it says,

> Bring ye all the tithes into the storehouse, that there may be meat in mine house, and *prove me now herewith*, saith the Lord of hosts, if I will not *open you the windows of heaven*, and *pour you out a blessing*, that there shall not be room enough to receive it.
>
> *And I will rebuke the devourer for your sakes*, and he shall not destroy the fruits of your ground; neither shall your vine cast her fruit before the time in the field, saith the Lord of hosts. (Malachi 3:10–11; italics added)

The Lord says to prove Him, to see if He will pour out blessings that we don't have room to receive. Do we believe that? Will we test that? Remember that the Lord is *bound* when we do what He says (D&C 89:10).

"But," you may say, "we pay tithing and still have money issues." That may be true, but not all blessings are in the form of a dollar. Often we overlook the daily abundance He has *already* given us. Children stay healthy, cars hold together, food is on the table, and clothes are on our backs. We're blessed with connections at work or opportunities for education. And we're inspired in choices that prevent future difficulties.

## A Generous Fast Offering

We are asked to fast once a month for two meals and to donate the amount of the meals as a fast offering to help the poor. So when it says a generous fast offering, just how much is generous?

President Spencer W. Kimball taught that the Lord would bless Church members if, according to their abilities, they doubled their fast offerings. We thus made it a point, even while students, to pay more than the cost of our meals as a fast offering. As our means have increased, we have increased our offerings, and the Lord has abundantly blessed us."[3]

We can teach our children to do the same. If desired, you can encourage your baptized children to donate a small amount, even a quarter, for people who struggle. Every little bit helps—not just financially, but in teaching children to focus less on the next video game and more on those in need.

It's helpful to share with our children where their donations go. H. David Burton stated that in 2007 alone, the Church responded to earthquakes in five countries, fires in six countries, starvation in eighteen countries, and the effects of severe storms in thirty-four countries. In all, about 170 major events, which came out to almost one every two days in the year.[4] This didn't include stats on rebuilding schools, vaccinating babies, training people in infant neonatal resuscitation, and much more.

Paying an honest tithe and a generous fast offering will bring us comfort and peace during difficult financial times. It will expand our resources so that we can more fully serve others.

Throughout my life, both single and married, these two basic principles have repeatedly blessed my life and the lives of those around me. Faithful obedience unties the Lord's hands and truly opens the windows of heaven.

## A Working Budget

Just the word "budget" can make people groan. Often because staying *within* a budget is the challenge, if not a seeming impossibility. Unaccounted-for expenses creep in each month—school fees, broken appliances, immunizations, and so on. Some financial analysts say we underestimate our budget by as much as $1400 a month.

What we need is a realistic working budget—easy to record and simple to track. Hotel owner J. W. Marriott once said that the company used a simple income/outgo ledger for years, and it worked beautifully. Keep it simple, make it real, and be consistent. That is a working budget.

First, choose your method—paper or computer. Elder Marvin J. Ashton gives a great one-sheet example in his pamphlet, "One for the Money"—an excellent investment for $1.95. I've written in a hardbound ledger, typed on a homemade computer form, and used a large envelope label affixed to my wallet with five major expense categories listed in columns. Computer and online budgeting software can be easy to use. Programs like YNAB, Mvelopes, and others not only allow you to track monthly spending but also help to discipline yourself for future financial goals.

After choosing a method, tracking is key. Choose a day of the week or month and take five or fifteen minutes to review your bank statement or checkbook. A quick look helps you make early adjustments and stay within limits.

## Back to Basics—Go!

If you haven't made a budget in the past year, try this quick exercise. Retrieve your last month's bank statement. On a sheet of paper, make two long columns—Income and Outgo, just like the Marriott ledger. *Quickly* go through the statement and highlight *income* categories—employment, gifts, or investments. Then review and highlight (in a different color) the statement for main *outgo* categories—tithes and offerings, groceries, house bills, gas, medical, recreation, fun food, and so on. Only use five to seven categories—all clearly defined, with no "miscellaneous" column. Assign every dollar a place.

Now calculate the amounts in each category (don't worry about writing place and date). Regardless of how unusual the month's expenses might be, this quick glance shows how your particular family spends.

Use this information to build your budget, with categories that fit your family. If you can, do the above exercise for three random months during the year (preferably your highest outgo times). With those numbers, estimate a realistic monthly budget and then add ten percent. Hold the worry—we will trim the budget in the next section.

## Savings

Ideally, we should save 15 percent of our income, but don't let that figure scare you. We can all start somewhere. One financial expert shared that a young woman decided to save only 5 dollars a day—the amount spent on a drink and a snack. This equaled about 35 dollars a week, which meant 150 dollars a month, which totaled to 2,000 dollars a year. If she invested that money at a growth rate of 11 percent, she would have accumulated 2 million dollars by age sixty-five. Even at less than this interest, she would still have a lovely nest egg.

## Back to Basics—Go!

Start small and try a money hunt. Search your home, car, and purse for loose change and gather it in a jar. We do these hunts occasionally in family home evening. Each child gets a resealable bag, and the race is on to find the change. All proceeds go in our Family Fund jar to be used for donation, bowling night, or school activities. You'll be surprised at the results. We've found as much as seventy-five dollars in one search—no small change.

So how else do you find money in your life? Try these two financial principles to save more money.

**1. Choose a money goal.** What's your ultimate financial goal? In order to change your money focus and habits, you must have a "dangling carrot" in front of your nose. What's *your* carrot—become debt-free, retire in comfort, go back to school, pay toward missions or college for children or grandchildren? Financial experts generally agree on a wise order of financial choices. I've reworked them to include religious essentials and called it a "Financial Snapshot."

| **Financial Snapshot** |
| --- |
| 1. Basic 3: tithe & fast offering, budget, savings |
| 2. Save $500 |
| 3. Eliminate consumer debt |
| 4. Insurances and Protection: auto/home, life, health, long-term disability, long-term care, will/estate planning |
| 5. Retirement |
| 6. Education and missions (for Mom and Dad too) |
| 7. Pay off home |
| 8. Pay off investments |
| 9. Create abundance; further "build the kingdom" |

Play around with this snapshot and create one that resonates with you. Evaluate where you are and what you need. Choose which item is key to your financial peace, then hone in on it like a laser beam. Involve your children and as a family, set the goal. Before eating out or seeing a movie in theaters, ask each other, "Does this help us meet our goal?"

For example, early in our marriage, my husband and I had decided to take our first trip to Disneyland with our two young children. We had enough savings to pay for the trip outright. We also had $1200 in credit card debt for a computer (back in the expensive days) and some necessary house items. Just before we bought trip tickets, we heard a man speak at church about growing up poor in India, and about gratitude and respect for money and things. He talked of opening the fridge and each time being amazed at the food ready to eat. He spoke about always being hungry as a child. At one point his friend, who was also starving, stole a piece of food. But a man caught him. As a punishment, the man cut off the boy's hand.

This talk affected us. Somehow the frills of Disneyland dissipated with the reality of an unpaid debt. We used the trip money to pay it off, and our focus since has been to remain consumer-debt free.

What is your personal money purpose? Once you know this, it will be easier to save.

TIP: If your focus is to be debt-free, try the helpful debt-elimination calendar in Elder Ashton's "One for the Money" pamphlet.

**2. Seek the savings.** Where is the money going each month? Look at your bank statement from the budget exercise and circle the amounts *not essential* to your money purpose. Calculate the total. Ask yourself the same questions as Elder Hales, who says that when faced with something to buy or do, you can learn to say, "We can't afford it," even if you can or if you simply want it.[5]

Years ago I analyzed our statement and expenses. Because we live in the mountains and drink eight gallons of milk a week, I had it delivered weekly. For family fun we would see a newly released movie. I bought conveniently packaged foods for school lunches.

After consideration, I made a few *simple* changes. I had the milk delivered every other week. Instead of buying treats, I baked twice a week. The last week of the month, I only shopped for essential groceries and used what we already had in the cupboards. We named one night a week "Food Storage Night" and made a meal from our active food storage pantry (the edible kind). Rather than see a newly released movie, we went to the dollar movies or rented one to view at home. After a month, I listed the amount we saved.

| Item | Money Saved |
|---|---|
| Delivered milk alternate weeks | 50.00 |
| Homemade treats | 45.00 |
| Essential-only grocery shopping one week | 150.00 |
| "Food Storage Night" once a week | 30.00 |
| Dollar movie for eight people | 60.00 |
| **Total Amount Saved** | **$335.00** |

Without fundamentally changing our quality of life, we saved over three hundred dollars a month. Your categories and reducing methods may be different, as well as the amount saved. But enjoy searching for ways to reduce *your* family's outgo. Utilize online sites that offer discounts, daily deals, or overstocked items for less money. Take a few minutes and find a better way to spend—or save the money outright.

Whatever method you choose, a minimal change in spending habits can likely create a surplus. Find it and then put it toward your financial purpose.

## Finances: Marriage

In marriage, finances are a two-person deal, and that means learning, growing, and compromising.

Elder Ashton says, "Control of the money by one spouse as a source of power and authority causes inequality in the marriage and is inappropriate. Conversely, if a marriage partner voluntarily removes himself or herself entirely from family financial management, that is an abdication of necessary responsibility."[6]

When my husband and I were first married, I asked about his ideal budget. He said, "Don't spend." As a couple, we may have different ideas on what a budget looks like, but we do have some basic counsel.

For men, the Lord has said: "And again, verily I say unto you, that every man who is obliged to provide for his own family, let him provide, and he shall in nowise lose his crown" (D&C 75:28). And from the Family Proclamation, we know that his job is mainly to provide.

Women are counseled that they "have claim on their husbands for their maintenance, until their husbands are taken" (D&C 83:2). Our main job, then, is to manage the money wisely. How do we go about merging the two roles?

**1. Have regular money talk.** Whether it's once a week, month, or quarter, take time to discuss your Financial Snapshot. Go through each item, note where you are in the process, and choose one financial goal for the next time period. Make it fun! Go to a park or out to eat—using one of your restaurant coupons—and enjoy the experience. You're building a financial future, so make it positive.

**2. Express appreciation.** One day I sent my husband a text from the grocery store, thanking him for making it easy to buy what we needed, worry-free. It was so meaningful to him that he shared it with a buddy. Thank your spouse for all he does to earn an income. Write a card, send an email, make a call, or simply say thanks. Often men only hear or see what's being spent. Post a sticky note on his computer or planner to show money that you've saved during the month. Help him to see your respect for his efforts to provide for the family.

**3. Get financially savvy.** Many women—even wives of financial experts—don't know money details. Do you know what life insurance you have and what the death benefits are? Do you have a list of all active accounts or loans and know if your name is on them?

Educate yourself. As Elder Ashton said, women cannot abdicate this responsibility to the husband. Understand terms and legal obligations—ignorance is not bliss. Whether you are a stay-at-home mother, work outside the home, or are somewhere in between, all women need to understand financial matters. A few minutes to comprehend them can save money immediately and stress later on.

Taking my own advice, one year I delved into the complex world of health insurance. After reviewing several policies—and the translations thereof—I discovered one plan that could ultimately save us over a thousand dollars a year. It took a little more time to manage but in the end was worth it.

## Back to Basics—Go!

Use the Financial Details chart below to record your information in one handy place. Do this exercise in chewable chunks! Take one item at a time. By doing one section a month, you will have a concise picture of your financial situation in just sixteen weeks. Place the sheet in your Home Binder for easy reference.

| **Financial Details** | |
|---|---|
| **Debts** | List all consumer debts, amounts, and contact information. |
| **Insurances and Protection** | Can include auto, home, life, health, long-term disability, long-term care, will and estate planning. List insurance companies, contact information, policy numbers, benefits, payments, and due dates. |
| **Accounts** | Saving, checking, retirement, college, and so on. List the account name and numbers, current amounts, interest rates, and beneficiaries. |
| **Investments** | List properties or assets, contact information, payments, interest rates, and performance |

Be savvy in daily money matters. Learn the cost of home and appliance repairs. Ask questions and equip yourself to negotiate better deals. When car shopping, if you know it's best to buy a two- to three-year old car for no more than $30,000 during December through February for lower prices, you're more prepared to negotiate with a salesperson or owner.

Be bold—ask, learn, and compare.

**4. Emotional triggers.** We all have them in some form. Hidden emotional catalysts that compel us to buy what we don't need or want—"retail therapy" run amok. If this is an issue for you or your spouse, consider agreeing to each use two shopping questions before you buy.

***A. Do we need it?*** One year, before back-to-school shopping, I asked my son if he needed shoes. He said yes and turned back to what he was doing. I started to write and then paused and asked again. "Do you really *need* new shoes?" This time he thought for a moment and said, "No." A thirty-second conversation saved me forty dollars.

Julie Morgenstern, author of *Organization Inside and Out*, reports that most people spend 15 to 20 percent of their yearly budget in repeat purchases that they *already have* or don't need. A few minutes to sort siblings' clothes or check the garage for a tool can save serious money.

***B. Do you love it?*** One day while shopping with my daughter, I saw that she was comparing the purchase of a necklace to her clothing budget. She liked the necklace, but I asked, "Do you *love* it?" Meaning, does it fit with what you need and hit home with a "Yes, this is it!"? After a moment, she said no and put it back. The necklace was never mentioned again (a good sign that it wasn't a keeper).

Other helpful tips can be to wait twenty-four hours—unless it makes better financial sense to buy immediately. You can set a shopping cap—either on amount (fifty dollars a month for recreational spending) or in time (children can purchase once a month). Or pay cash only, which automatically limits what you spend.

Choose one of these four principles and enjoy creating more financial peace this week.

## Finances: Teach Your Children

Regardless of age, it's never too late to teach children about money value and management. Our example teaches them every day.

Elder M. Russell Ballard told of a family friend who travels frequently with extended family. She said that parents are vital examples for their children, noting on the trips that if the mothers were frugal then so were the daughters.[7]

As we explain key principles and model good practices in work, money value, and abundance, our children will be better prepared, now and for the future.

## Work

As parents, just because we *can* afford to buy something, doesn't mean we should. Elder H. David Burton acknowledged that well-to-do parents have a tough time saying no. But in saying yes to everything, they make it more difficult for their children to learn about hard work and delayed gratification.

"Parents who have been successful in acquiring more often have a difficult time saying no. . . . Their children run the risk of not learning important values like hard work, delayed gratification, honesty, and compassion."[8]

Consider the cost of sports, dance, or music camps; book orders; new electronics; clothes; and more. Help children understand a clear reality—there is no free ride. It is their work and their glory to get good grades and complete chores. As a child, these constitute their "day job." Understanding this not only gives children purpose, it also teaches them discipline and value at an early age.

In our family, a grade of C or lower is not okay (mainly because all of the children so far are capable of doing better). When our son got a few C grades due to admitted laziness, he became our yard boy for the summer. Through this experience, he understood—day after day—the reality of cutting corners in a "job" and the resulting labor level.

This consequence sounds harsh—and *must* be done with love—but it is so valuable in their youth.

As our children do their "day jobs," we can give perks, and, just like in the real world, parents can reward saving. If possible, match their deposits. The same principle can apply to withdrawals—it would include the matched sum returned to the parents. This is a great incentive for children to do extra chores for desired items rather than pull from savings.

As you teach these real-world concepts, it empowers children. I remember when one of my daughters got the concept of earning her own money. When she was six years old, she regularly approached me about ordering books from a school flyer. I told her we weren't paying for book orders at that time but that she could do jobs to *earn* the money. She stood still, and I could almost see a lightbulb over her head. "You mean, I can do a job and get money and buy the book?" I said yes. She folded laundry and matched socks, each time calculating her earnings. This experience ended the monthly book order debate.

Regarding what we pay our children to do, first consider what is part of being a contributing family member and what is extra earnings. Perhaps children are not paid for regular good grades, but anything above that could become a bonus—extra cash, a new outfit, or a fun day out. Some things are expected—just like at a workplace—and other things are extra-mile efforts.

## Value

Sometimes parents complain that their children ask for too much, too often, with too little respect. But we as parents might forget to teach our children the value of a dollar or what it costs to run a home, drive a car, or maintain a family.

For a fun family home evening activity, try a Monopoly budget game. First, ask the children to list their perceived budget categories (for example, rent/mortgage, food, gasoline for the car) and the amount of money needed for each category to run a home each month. Show them how it compares to the actual expenses. Then, tell them the actual income (or a pretend sum) for one month. Assign each child a budget category and hand them their initial perceived budget amount in play money. Compare the perceived to the actual, and what they could do to fix the difference. This experience can help them see the importance of a budget, the difference between perceived and actual expenses, and why it's important not to waste the milk.

Teaching children about money can be fun and easy. Have your children help pay monthly bills occasionally; walk them through an online system or record it on a budget sheet. In their recreational spending, show them how to compare prices by checking reputable online ads, consumer protection sites, and so on. While grocery shopping, explain unit prices or when to pay for quality versus getting a discount deal.

Understanding the value of money changes their spending habits. One of our sons wanted hobby air gun gear, but the price was steep and he was using his own funds. He chose to shop at a thrift store for the clothing, use old karate boxing pads for protection, and apply some duct tape to make an "armor" plating (that actually worked). For a few dollars he was able to create a usable substitution and save money for something else.

## Abundance

When we recognize how much we have, we're able to give easily and with joy.

Elder Hales shared that often we feel embarrassed if we have less than the neighbors, which prompts us to go into debt for unnecessary things. As we live in this cycle, depression and low self-esteem can result, which affects our relationships, including our relationship with the Lord, and ultimately leaves us with less time and desire for spiritual matters.[9]

In our day, fewer children and adults are thinking how they can create abundance for others. We can teach our children to serve—to think of those who are in need. We can teach them how they can help in simple ways.

Before you cart off old clothes to the thrift store, check your neighborhood for children in need. Elder Ashton encourages children to donate to their siblings' mission funds.[10] From fast offerings to scout projects to school fund-raisers, we can help our children step outside of what they want and consider those less fortunate.

One Christmas, my husband and I had chosen to take the children to Disneyland. (Will we ever get there?) Before purchasing the tickets, we found out that a family in our neighborhood was in need. I remember walking into our bedroom where our children were all folding laundry during laundry day. I said, "Here's the deal: we were going to surprise you with a trip to Disneyland for Christmas. But we just found out that a family is struggling. How would you feel about using that money to help them?" Without missing a beat, they all said things like, "Sure," "No problem," "Well, yeah." I got teary-eyed. It wasn't so much that they would agree to it—children generally want to help those in need. It was that they didn't consider it a loss.

Children's responses may not always be this clear-cut or positive—we've experienced a wide variety. But giving our children opportunities to serve may surprise us—and them.

## Wrapping Up

Simple principles and practices for yourself, family, and children can bring financial peace and abundance. As we remember the purpose of money and wealth, we understand better how to use them. Elder Joseph B. Wirthlin said:

> How can we ever repay the debt we owe to the Savior? He paid a debt He did not owe to free us from a debt we can never pay. Because of Him, we will live forever. Because of Him our sins can be swept away. . . . We have earthly debts and heavenly debts. Let us be wise in dealing with each of them. . . . "Lay not up for yourselves treasures upon earth, where moth and rust doth corrupt, and where thieves break through and steal. But lay up for yourselves treasures in heaven." The riches of this world are as dust compared to the riches that await the faithful in the mansions of our Heavenly Father.[11]

## Suggested Goals for Establishing Financial Peace and Prosperity

### *Finances: Self*

- Consider your fast offering and research quotes from Church leaders. Determine a figure that feels right for you and your situation.
- Create a simple working budget using the suggestions in this chapter.
- Do a quick money hunt in your home or apartment. Use the change for something purposeful.
- Create a Financial Snapshot.

### *Finances: Marriage*

- Choose a regular monthly or weekly time to discuss financial matters.
- Write a thank you note to your spouse for all he does to provide for the family.
- Create a Financial Details record.
- Identify emotional triggers with money and choose a healthy behavior to replace them with.

### *Finances: Children*

- Consider an item that your child wants. Discuss ways that he or she can earn the money to buy it.
- Help your children find ways to donate small earned amounts to a worthy cause.
- Have a gratitude Family Home Evening. List all the things that you and your family are grateful for and then secretly serve someone in the neighborhood.

## Notes


Quote at chapter start found in Marvin J. Ashton, *One for the Money: Guide to Family Finance* (Salt Lake City: The Church of Jesus Christ of Latter-day Saints, 2006), 1.

1. Ibid.
2. Joseph B. Wirthlin, "The Straight and Narrow Way," *Ensign*, Nov. 1990, 65.
3. Gordon B. Hinckley, "To the Boys and to the Men," *Ensign*, Nov. 1998, 67.
4. H. David Burton, "And Who Is My Neighbor?," *Ensign*, May 2008, 51–52.
5. Robert D. Hales, "Becoming Provident Providers Temporally and Spiritually," *Ensign*, May 2009, 7–10.
6. Ashton, *One for the Money*, 3.
7. M. Russell Ballard, "Mothers and Daughters," *Ensign*, May 2010, 18–21.
8. H. David Burton, "More Holiness Give Me," *Ensign*, Nov. 2004, 98–100.
9. Hales, "Becoming Provident Providers," 7–10.
10. Ashton, *One for the Money*, 9.
11. Joseph B. Wirthlin, "Earthly Debts, Heavenly Debts," *Ensign*, May 2004, 40–43.

# back to basics

## *Final Thoughts*

You've read, studied, applied, and succeeded. Or you're about to. No matter where you are in *Faithful, Fit, and Fabulous*, I invite you not to be overwhelmed. This book contains a great deal of information, and you may be tempted to try it all at once. Please don't! Build "line upon line, precept upon precept" (2 Nephi 28:30), and you *will* create a joyful and purposeful life.

Remember to follow the program protocol: read one chapter a week and complete the Back to Basics—Go! suggestions *as you desire*. Set one goal a week and use your best energy to achieve it. Review your efforts at the end of the week and make any adjustments. Enjoy your reward and celebrate your success, big or small!

Step by step you will feel and see changes. Keep your overall life plan at the forefront and then continue to set, achieve, review, and reward your goal each week. Do this for eight weeks and then take a break to focus on maintaining your progress.

As I mentioned before, if you have any questions, feel free to email me at connie@8basics.com.

I wish you great joy and success using the principles and practices in *Faithful, Fit, and Fabulous*. Learn what excites you, set goals that move you, and enjoy every step of the way!

# back to basics

## *More!*

**What are Post-It Pages and how do I use them?**

The Post-It Page is a simple way to record and post your life paragraph, Weekly Goal, and reward. At the end of the week, you can complete the review questions to better understand what worked, what didn't, and what you want to do differently on the next week's goal for greater success. I recommend that you keep these sheets in a personal binder to track your progress.

An original Post-It Page is provided for you to copy directly from the book. Or you can visit www.8basics.com for a free download. A sample completed Post-It Page is included here for you to see a finished copy.

**What is your website address and what will I find there?**

Visit www.8basics.com for tips, products, and a weekly blog to support your goal success! Each week I share a motivational tip on a chapter topic and insights on my blog. You can read my *Deseret News* columns and excerpts from the books *Life Is Too Short for One Hair Color*, *Life Is Too Short for Sensible Shoes*, and *Are You Ready for a LIFEChange?*. If you want a live presentation, you'll find my speaking or book signing schedule. For product information, the website provides audio segments from talk CDs and text samples from books. Feel free to post any questions or suggestions.

## Post-It Page: ____________________

Write your Weekly Goal. Include how often, how long, and on what days. Post on your wall. At the end of the week, enjoy a reward and complete the review.

### My Life Paragraph

______________________________________________

______________________________________________

______________________________________________

______________________________________________

______________________________________________

______________________________________________

### My Weekly Goal

I will ______________________________________

### My Reward!

I will enjoy _________________________________

### Review

Consider the past week. Answer the following to create a new goal.

1. **On a scale of 1 to 10 (1=low, 10=high), rate your week's success:**
2. **What worked?**
3. **What didn't work?**
4. **What will you do differently in the coming week?**

**Great job!**

## SAMPLE Post-It Page: Create a Life Plan

Write your Weekly Goal—include how often, how long, and on what days. Post on your wall. At the end of the week, enjoy a reward and complete the review.

### My Life Paragraph

I am a loving, spiritually centered, happy daughter of God. I enjoy a personal and creative purpose. I connect with family and friends through healthy, positive interactions and communications. I know how to deal with difficult situations and set appropriate boundaries. I am financially savvy—wisely spending, saving, tracking, and organizing money matters. I balance and organize time and home efficiently and teach my children life skills. I make time for hobbies and fun and delight in serving others.

### My Weekly Goal

I will read or listen to scriptures (conference CDs), for 15 mins. on Mon/Wed/Fri by 9 a.m.

### My Reward!

I will enjoy a hot bubble bath with lavender salts while listening to quiet music.

### Review

Consider the past week and answer the following to create a new goal.

1. **On a scale of 1 to 10 (1=low, 10=high), rate your week's success:** 10
2. **What worked?** Putting the scriptures on my bedstand and conference CDs in the car on Sunday for the week; choosing a study topic (patience); doing one more time than planned; taking a lovely bubble bath.
3. **What didn't work?** Getting up late on Wednesday and forgetting on Friday until the afternoon.
4. **What will you do differently in the coming week?** Put a sticky note on my planner and in the car to remind me.

**Great job!**

# back to basics

## *Power Week!*

Perhaps, after successfully completing a goal from each chapter, you are ready for something more challenging. Or you're already successfully setting Weekly Goals and want a jump start in several areas.

Enter the Power Week.

In one week, I challenge you to accomplish one goal in each of the eight Back to Basics areas.

Before you do this, I recommend that you have finished at least one goal in each area, one week at a time, for a total of eight completed goals.

To begin, use the sample Power Week chart provided and refer as needed to the completed chart from one of my Power Weeks. Your goal is to be at a 9 or 10 completion rating for each goal during the week. If you make an 8 rating, that is still great work.

Prayerfully consider what would be ideal one-week goals in each topic area. List them in the Goal column. Consult your weekly schedule and pencil in the days and times you think most likely to fit with achieving particular goals. For example, perhaps the fitness goal would be best in the morning, the organizing goal when the children are napping, and the joy in womanhood goal on Saturday morning.

Mix up the goals with one-time projects and lifestyle habits. That way you're not trying to establish eight new habits, just complete eight important goals.

Pick a daily time to review your goals. It isn't necessary to work on one goal per day or at the same time or in the same way. You can accomplish most of them at the beginning of the week and save a few for the end, or vice versa. You decide! A Power Week is about daily evaluating what you want to accomplish, writing it down, and making it happen in the best way for you and your family.

As you accomplish a goal, write the outcome on the chart and then rate the degree of success on a scale from 1 to 10 (1 for not completed in any way, 10 for 100-percent completion). At the week's end, use the review at the bottom of the chart to note what worked, what didn't, and what you will do differently next time. Then put this sheet in your personal binder.

Because a Power Week takes more structure and energy, you will need to plan ahead. Don't add in extraneous activities or events. Stay laser-beam focused on your goals. Involve your family and enlist their help.

Caveat: Do not do Power Weeks consecutively—I recommend about once a quarter. This is a spring cleaning goal-setting week. You can roll up your sleeves and get a whole lot done but only for that week. Afterward, savor your accomplishment and then return to the normal one-goal a week plan (which will seem like a breeze!) Remember, there is to be an opposite in all things, so after the big push, allow a soft letdown. This will bring you more peace, sanity, and success.

## My Experience with a Power Week

As you'll note from my completed Power Week chart, I chose a mixture of one-time goals (create a life board, prepare kids' cookbook, review our budget) and on-going lifestyle goals (attend the temple, Friday Fun, chore follow-up). Different goals required varying energy, structure, and time increments.

Making your plan realistic is key to an enjoyable and successful Power Week. Family is still your focus, so work with the curve balls that life brings you and adjust! You'll note that on my chart, I rated my life board a "9." I had planned to complete it on a relaxing Sunday, the last night of my Power Week. To prepare for it, I had already gathered my chosen cutouts and stickers and typed my goals, dreams, and other information. Everything was set. All that remained was to glue the items on the board.

And then, of course, Sunday was anything but relaxing. By the time I returned home for the evening from my last meeting, the children wanted to spend family time playing a "Sunday Scrabble" tournament (scripture words are double!). I debated. Was this the time to be stalwart and official (knowing I would use this week as an example for the book), or to be with my family? I consciously chose to be with my family, knowing that this would be a better example overall rather than pushing to complete something that could be done just as well the next afternoon. So I rated myself at a 9 because I planned ahead and completed most of the project, setting a goal to finish it the next day, which I did.

In rating your own goal-achieving efforts, don't focus too much on the minutia of the exact number. You're looking for patterns to tell you which goals or habits work, which don't, and why or why not. If you completed a goal about 80 percent, then write down an 8; if you only finished 50 percent, put down a 5. It's not a race or a competition. This growth is between you and Heavenly Father, and no one else.

Be realistic, be wise, and remember that goals are not to inhibit your quality of life but to improve it.

| **Back to Basics—Power Week!** | | | |
|---|---|---|---|
| **Area** | **Goal** | **Outcome** | **1–10** |
| **Goal 1:**<br>**Holy Habits** | Attend the temple | Didn't wait until Saturday, did early in week | 10! |
| **Goal 2:**<br>**Create a Life Plan** | Create my life board 2011 | Cutouts ready to go; chose to finish Monday | 9 |
| **Goal 3:**<br>**Discover More Joy in Womanhood** | Friday Fun! | Zumba, relax, movies, ice cream, read | 10! |
| **Goal 4:**<br>**Feel Fit and Fabulous** | Sugar only on weekend | Kept treats for Friday; didn't bake during week | 10! |
| **Goal 5:**<br>**Find Balance in Motherhood** | Chore follow-up | Better motivation, followed through, stayed calm | 10! |
| **Goal 6:**<br>**Get Organized! Family** | Prepare kids' cookbook | Did all meals and desserts, ready for lamination | 10! |
| **Goal 7:**<br>**Create Healthy Connections: Marriage** | Positive reminders | Creative solutions to remind D. no phone at meals | 10! |
| **Goal 8:**<br>**Financial Peace: Self** | Review 2011 budget | Only took 20 mins. to review prior one and adjust | 10! |

**REWARD:** Buy a new writing chair for my desk area!
**Overall Results 1–10:** 10!

## Review:

**What worked?** The Power Week helped me stay focused and keep on it until each goal was accomplished, despite distractions.

**What didn't?** Spending unplanned time on critiquing someone's book—it made me have to squish achieving some of the goals and therefore made them more stressful to accomplish. Next time maybe scale back one or two of the goals and adjust!

**What should be changed?** Keep basically the same except next time know earlier in the week more specifically what I want to accomplish.

| Back to Basics—Power Week! | | | |
|---|---|---|---|
| **Area** | **Goal** | **Outcome** | **1–10** |
| **Goal 1: Holy Habits** | | | |
| **Goal 2: Create a Life Plan** | | | |
| **Goal 3: Discover More Joy in Womanhood** | | | |
| **Goal 4: Feel Fit and Fabulous** | | | |
| **Goal 5: Find Balance in Motherhood** | | | |
| **Goal 6: Get Organized!** | | | |
| **Goal 7: Create Healthy Connections** | | | |
| **Goal 8: Financial Peace** | | | |

**REWARD:**
**Overall Results 1–10:**

## Review:

**What worked?**

**What didn't?**

**What should be changed?**

# bibliography

Ashton, Marvin J. *One for the Money: Guide to Family Finance* (Salt Lake City: The Church of Jesus Christ of Latter-day Saints, 2006).

Ballard, M. Russell. "Daughters of God." *Ensign*, May 2008, 108–10.

———. "Mothers and Daughters." *Ensign*, May 2010, 18–21.

Banchek, Linda. *The Ayurveda Cookbook: Cooking for Life*. Fairfield, IA: Orchids & Herbs Press, 1990.

Beck, Julie B. "And upon the Handmaids in Those Days Will I Pour Out My Spirit." *Ensign*, May 2010, 10–12.

———. BYU Women's Conference, opening session, April 29, 2010.

Burton, H. David. "And Who Is My Neighbor?" *Ensign*, May 2008, 51–52.

———. "More Holiness Give Me." *Ensign*, Nov. 2004, 98–100.

Chapman, Gary. *The Five Love Languages of Children*. Chicago: Northfield Publishing, 2005.

Christofferson, D. Todd. "Reflections on a Consecrated Life." *Ensign*, Nov. 2010, 16–19.

Clegg, Gayle M. "The Finished Story." *Ensign*, May 2004, 15.

Condie, Spencer J. "Claim the Exceeding Great and Precious Promises." *Ensign*, Nov. 2007, 16.

Coopersmith, Geralyn. *Fit and Female*. Hoboken: John Wiley & Sons, 2006.

Dew, Sheri L. *If Life Were Easy, It Wouldn't Be Hard*. Salt Lake City: Deseret Book, 2005.

———. *No Doubt about It.* Salt Lake City: Deseret Book, 2001.

———. "We Are Women of God." *Ensign*, Nov. 1999, 97.

Dibb, Ann M. "Hold On." *Ensign*, Nov. 2009, 79–81.

Edmunds, Mary Ellen. *You Can Never Get Enough of What You Don't Need: The Quest for Contentment.* Salt Lake City: Deseret Book, 2005.

Eyring, Henry B. "A Discussion on Scripture Study," *Ensign*, July 2005, 22.

———. *To Draw Closer to God.* Salt Lake: Deseret Book, 1997.

Faust, James E. "A Message to My Granddaughters: Becoming 'Great Women.'" *Ensign*, Sept. 1986, 16.

———. "Obedience: The Path to Freedom." *Ensign*, May 1999, 47.

First Presidency letter, 11 Feb. 1999. Cited in *Church News*, 27 Feb. 1999.

Gottman, John. *The Seven Principles for Making Marriage Work.* New York: Three Rivers Press, 1999.

Greenspan, Stanley. *The Challenging Child.* New York: Addison-Wesley, 1995.

Hafen, Bruce C. "Covenant Marriage." *Ensign*, Nov. 1996, 26.

Hales, Robert D. "Becoming Provident Providers Temporally and Spiritually." *Ensign*, May 2009, 7–10.

———. "Couple Missionaries: Blessings from Sacrifice and Service." *Ensign*, May 2005, 39–42.

———. "With All the Feeling of a Tender Parent: A Message of Hope to Families." *Ensign*, May 2004, 90.

Hinckley, Gordon B. "To the Boys and to the Men." *Ensign*, Nov. 1998, 67.

Hinckley, Marjorie Pay. *Small and Simple Things.* Salt Lake City: Deseret Book, 1999.

Holland, Jeffrey R. "To Young Women." *Ensign*, Oct. 2005, 28–30.

Holland, Jeffrey R. and Patricia T. Holland. *On Earth as It Is in Heaven.* Salt Lake City: Deseret Book, 1989.

Jones, Barbara Barrington. *The Confident You*. Salt Lake City: Deseret Book, 1992.

Kikuchi, Yoshihiko. "Opening the Heavens." *Ensign*, Aug. 2009, 34–38.

Lant, Cheryl C. "My Soul Delighteth in the Scriptures." *Ensign*, Nov. 2005, 76.

———. "Righteous Traditions." *Ensign*, May 2008, 13–14.

Larsen, Sharon. *All Rain, No Mud: Simple Secrets for Happiness Even on Rainy Days*. Salt Lake City: Deseret Book, 2005.

Lee, Harold B. "Love at Home." Chap. 14 in *Teachings of Presidents of the Church: Harold B. Lee*. Salt Lake City: The Church of Jesus Christ of Latter-day Saints, 2000.

Lewis, C.S. "The Weight of Glory" (preached originally as a sermon in the Church of St Mary the Virgin, Oxford, on June 8, 1942), published in *Theology*, Nov. 1941, and by the S.P.C.K, 1942.

Lundberg, Gary and Joy. *I Don't Have to Make Everything All Better*. New York: Penguin Putnam, 1995.

Malm, Per G. "Rest unto Your Souls." *Ensign*, Nov. 2010, 102.

Matsumori, Vicki B. "Helping Others Recognize the Whisperings of the Spirit." *Ensign*, Nov. 2009, 10–12.

Miller, Wiley. *Why We'll Never Understand Each Other*. Kansas City, MO: Andrews McMeel, 2003.

Monson, Thomas S. "To the Rescue." *Ensign*, May 2001, 48.

———. "Your Eternal Voyage." *Ensign*, May 2000, 41.

Oaks, Dallin H. "Adversity." *Ensign*, July 1998, 7.

———. "The Challenge to Become." *Ensign*, Nov. 2000, 32–34.

———. "Good, Better, Best." *Ensign*, Nov. 2007, 104–8.

Okazaki, Chieko N. *Lighten Up*. Salt Lake City: Deseret Book, 1993.

Packer, Boyd K. *Memorable Stories and Parables by Boyd K. Packer*. Salt Lake City: Bookcraft, 1997.

Perry, L. Tom. "Fatherhood, an Eternal Calling." *Ensign*, May 2004, 69–72.

Renlund, Dale G. "Preserving the Heart's Mighty Change." *Ensign*, Nov. 2009, 98–99.

Scott, Richard G. "To Acquire Spiritual Guidance." *Ensign*, Nov. 2009, 6–9.

———. "Using the Supernal Gift of Prayer," *Ensign*, May 2007, 8–11.

Skinner, Andrew C. *Temple Worship: 20 Truths That Will Bless Your Life*. Salt Lake City: Deseret Book, 2007.

Somers, Suzanne. *Ageless*. New York: Crown Publishers, 2006.

Stoddard, Alexandra. *Daring to Be Yourself.* New York: Avon Books, 1990.

Tribole, Evelyn and Elyse Resch. *Intuitive Eating.* New York: St. Martin's Press, 1995.

Uchtdorf, Dieter F. "Happiness, Your Heritage." *Ensign*, Nov. 2008, 117–20.

Wirthlin, Joseph B. "The Abundant Life." *Ensign*, May 2006, 99–102.

———. "Earthly Debts, Heavenly Debts." *Ensign*, May 2004, 40–43.

———. "The Straight and Narrow Way," *Ensign*, Nov. 1990, 65.

# about the author

Connie E. Sokol is a mother of six, a national and local presenter, and a regular speaker at BYU Education Week. She is a former TV and radio host and columnist for *Deseret News*. Despite having her hands full, and with her left toe, she has recorded several talk CDs and authored *Life Is Too Short for One Hair Color* and *Life Is Too Short for Sensible Shoes*. Mrs. Sokol delights in time spent with her family and eating decadent treats.